Monitoring of Retrogressive Thaw Slumps in the Arctic Network, 2011

Three-dimensional modeling of landform change

Natural Resource Report NPS/ARCN/NRDS—2012/247

David K. Swanson

National Park Service
Fairbanks Administrative Center
4175 Geist Rd.
Fairbanks, AK 99709

February 2012

U.S. Department of the Interior
National Park Service
Natural Resource Stewardship and Science
Fort Collins, Colorado

The National Park Service, Natural Resource Stewardship and Science office in Fort Collins, Colorado publishes a range of reports that address natural resource topics of interest and applicability to a broad audience in the National Park Service and others in natural resource management, including scientists, conservation and environmental constituencies, and the public.

The Natural Resource Data Series is intended for the timely release of basic data sets and data summaries. Care has been taken to assure accuracy of raw data values, but a thorough analysis and interpretation of the data has not been completed. Consequently, the initial analyses of data in this report are provisional and subject to change.

All manuscripts in the series receive the appropriate level of peer review to ensure that the information is scientifically credible, technically accurate, appropriately written for the intended audience, and designed and published in a professional manner.

Data in this report were collected and analyzed using methods based on established, peer-reviewed protocols and were analyzed and interpreted within the guidelines of the protocols.

Views, statements, findings, conclusions, recommendations, and data in this report do not necessarily reflect views and policies of the National Park Service, U.S. Department of the Interior. Mention of trade names or commercial products does not constitute endorsement or recommendation for use by the U.S. Government.

This report is available from the National Park Service, Arctic Inventory and Monitoring Network (http://science.nature.nps.gov/im/units/arcn/) and the Natural Resource Publications Management website (http://www.nature.nps.gov/publications/nrpm/).

Please cite this publication as:

Swanson, D. K. 2012. Monitoring of retrogressive thaw slumps in the Arctic Network, 2011: Three-dimensional modeling of landform change. Natural Resource Data Series NPS/ARCN/NRDS—2012/247. National Park Service, Fort Collins, Colorado.

NPS 965/112838,February 2012

Contents

Contents (continued)

Figures

Tables

Abstract

Retrogressive thaw slumps (RTS) are caused by thaw of massive ground ice on slopes and combine subsidence, mass movement, and water erosion. They can expose several hectares of bare soil that is susceptible to erosion into nearby water bodies. In the summers of 2010 and 2011, oblique aerial-photographs of 26 RTS in Noatak National Preserve (NOAT) and Gates of the Arctic National Park and Preserve (GAAR) were taken with a hand-held, 35-mm digital camera. Accurate ground control was obtained at 23 of the slumps by surveying the location of temporary targets that were captured on the aerial photographs and then removed. These photographs were used to create high-resolution three-dimensional topographic models with photographic overlay. Photographs were taken in both years at 18 of the RTS. The current report: 1) documents changes in the slumps that had photographs from both years, and 2) describes a new slump photographed for the first time in 2011.

Study slumps ranged in area from less than 1 to about 5 ha. The change in area of individual slumps between 2010 to 2011 ranged from negligible amounts to about 1 ha. Main scarp migration rates in slumps with vertical main scarps and exposed massive ice ranged from 10 to 65 m between late June 2010 and mid July 2011. The most rapid scarp migration was by a process here called "fall and flow", where turf and sediments blocks fell down the near-vertical scarp and mostly disintegrated or sank into the liquefied mud below. Less active slumps grew by a scarp migration process called "extensional flow", where long fractures developed parallel to the main scarp, no massive ice was exposed, and many elongate blocks of turf survived the trip down the main scarp. Scarp migration by extensional flow was less than 20 m between the two years and in some cases less than 5 m.

Most subsidence occurred in the new part of the slump (between the positions of the main scarps in the two years'). The volume of subsidence was over 30,000 m^3 in the most active slump. The newly subsided area typically consisted of liquefied mud that would not support a person's weight. Below the subsidence area in the active slumps was a zone of firmer ground up to 50 m wide where the surface rose one or two meters between the two years. The volume of subsidence was usually several times as great as the volume gained in the zone of surface rise immediately below. The net volume lost was probably mainly water from melted ice that ran off, but also probably included some material eroded away by running water. However, none of the slumps showed major changes in their lower parts, beyond minor growth in vegetation and minor changes in small runoff channels.

Acknowledgments

Thanks to C. Priest and K. Hill for help in the field. J. Lawler and D. Capps provided helpful comments on the manuscript.

Introduction

Retrogressive thaw slumps (RTS) are dramatic features of the arctic landscape caused by thaw of permafrost. They occur where a cut-bank in ice-rich permafrost advances into undisturbed ground as material thaws in the steep bank, falls or slides onto the adjacent more gentle slope, and then is transported away by viscous flow or water erosion (Burn and Lewkowicz 1990). The advancing cut-bank, referred to here as the "main scarp" in keeping with standard landslide terminology (Beltran et al. 1993), is typically 2 to 10 m high, though it may reach 35 m (Crosby 2009). RTS often begin as escarpments produced by coastal, lakeshore, or fluvial erosion and then advance away from the shore by thaw and slumping. Very ice-rich material of substantial thickness (e.g., several meters) and lateral extent is needed to produce a RTS (Lacelle et al. 2010).

Because RTS are large erosion features that often occur near water bodies, they can affect water quality. Suspended sediment, ions in solution, and pH have been shown to be higher below RTS and other thermokarst erosion features (Bowden et al. 2008, Crosby 2009, Kokelj et al. 2005). Ions that increase include nutrient species such as potassium, phosphate, sulfate, ammonium, and nitrate, as well as other common soil cations such as calcium, magnesium, and sodium.

While localized thaw and refreezing of permafrost occurs under a stable cold arctic climate, climate change has been cited as a cause of increased thaw of permafrost since 1982 in Alaska (Jorgenson et al. 2006). Concerns about the future state of permafrost led the National Park Service Arctic Inventory and Monitoring Network (ARCN, the five NPS units in northern and western Alaska) to include permafrost as a monitoring "vital sign" (Lawler et al. 2009). Thaw-related slumping and associated soil erosion may have increased in ARCN in recent years (Balser et al. 2007), and the activity of RTS in some areas of Canada has increased in recent decades (Lantuit and Pollard 2008, Lantz and Kokelj 2008).

In 2010 ARCN initiated a monitoring program for retrogressive thaw slumps (Swanson and Hill 2010). High-resolution three-dimensional (3-D) models of selected slumps were produced from oblique 35 mm aerial photographs together with surveyed ground control. Most of the slumps imaged in 2010 were re-photographed in 2011, and additional ground control was obtained where it was lacking in 2010. The present report uses the data from 2010 and 2011 to document the growth of these RTS through comparison of topographic models and orthophotographs from the two years.

Methods

Study Area and Site Selection

RTS were selected from mapping of permafrost-related erosion features in ARCN (Swanson 2012 and unpublished data for Gates of the Arctic National Park and Preserve) and previous work by Balser et al. (2007)(Fig. 1, Table 1). RTS were selected for intensive photographic monitoring based on 1) size, 2) potential for siltation of adjacent water bodies, 3) potential for encroachment on archeological sites, 4) visual impact, and 5) proximity to other slumps (for economy of access).

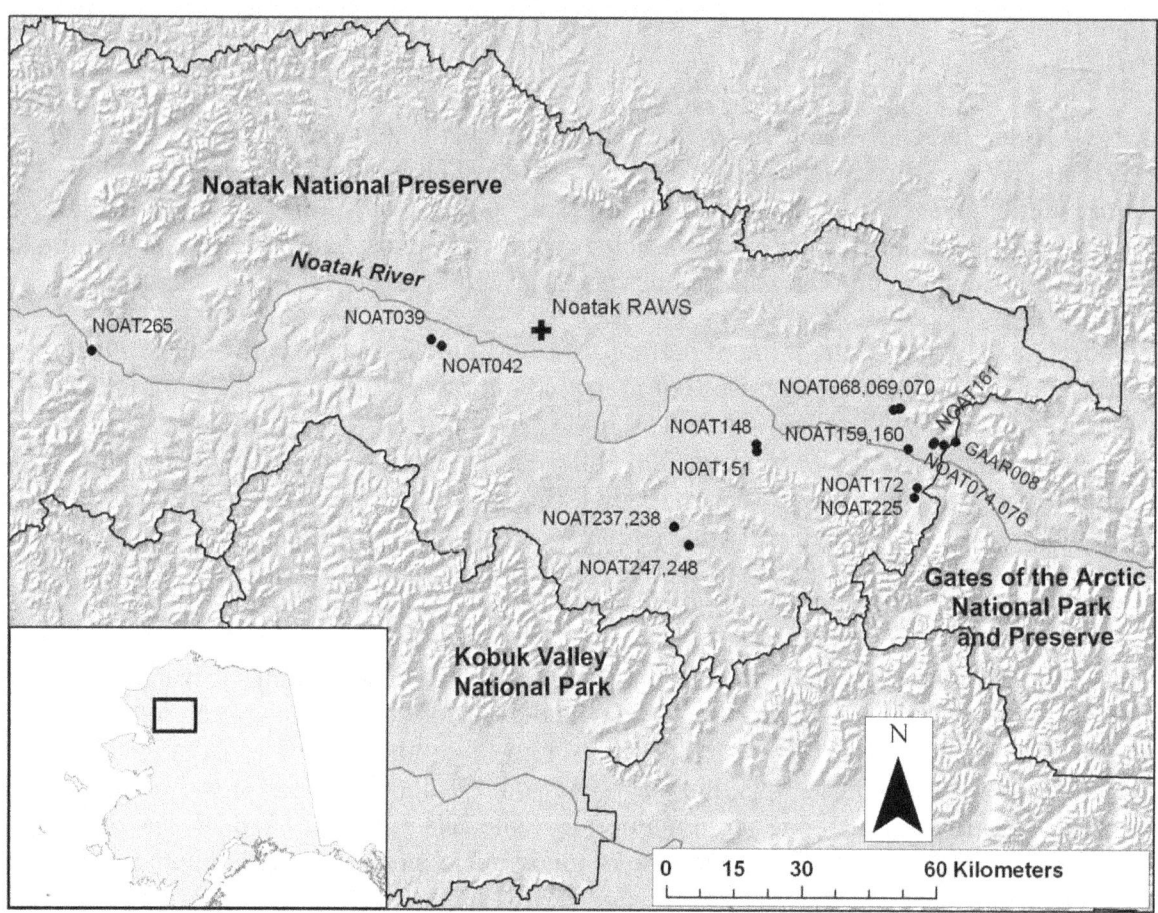

Figure 1. Locations of the retrogressive thaw slumps described in this report. For a comprehensive list of all slumps with monitoring data, see Table 1.

All of the study RTS are within the zone of continuous permafrost (Jorgenson et al. 2008). Vegetation in NOAT is dominantly arctic tundra, with trees occurring at low elevations and mainly in the western part of the Preserve; of the slumps treated in this report, only NOAT265 has trees on the adjacent slopes (balsam poplar *Populus balsamifera* and a few hybrid birch *Betula* sp.). Data from the Noatak RAWS shows a January mean temperature of -25.3 °C, July mean of 13.3 °C, and annual mean of -7.9 °C (WRCC 2011; for the period 1990-2011 with occasional missing values, mainly in the winter). This station is in the east-central part of the Preserve, in an area of tundra vegetation (Fig. 1). At the Kelly RAWS, the Jan mean is -18.5 °C, July 13.9 °C, annual -4.1 °C (WRCC 2011; for the period 1990-2011 with winter months largely missing prior to 1998). The Kelly RAWS is in the far western part of the Preserve, in a low-elevation forested area (50 km due west of NOAT265 in Fig. 1).

Table 1. Retrogressive thaw slumps monitored by ARCN

Slump identifier	Longitude, deg-min W (NAD83)	Latitude, deg-min N (NAD83)	Fieldwork[1]		Analyzed in this report[2]
			2010	2011	
GAAR008	156° 29.17'	67° 54.04'	s	s	√
GAAR010	154° 40.81'	68° 22.99'	s	-	
NOAT004	159° 14.65'	68° 04.22'	p	-	
NOAT037	161° 52.40'	67° 59.17'	-	s	
NOAT039	159° 17.48'	68° 02.15'	s	-	√
NOAT042	159° 14.08'	68° 01.43.'	s	-	√
NOAT068	156° 47.30'	67° 57.66'	s	p	√
NOAT069	156° 47.56'	67° 57.64'	s	p	√
NOAT070	156° 49.42'	67° 57.50'	s	p	√
NOAT071	156° 48.02'	67° 56.56'	s	-	
NOAT072	156° 48.40'	67° 56.62'	p	-	
NOAT073	156° 49.14'	67° 56.85'	p	-	
NOAT074	156° 36.03'	67° 53.87.'	p	s	√
NOAT076	156° 36.27'	67° 53.66'	p	s	√
NOAT148	157° 31.94'	67° 52.61'	s	p	√
NOAT151	157° 31.60'	67° 51.77'	s	s	√
NOAT159	156° 44.15'	67° 52.98'	p	s	√
NOAT160	156° 44.12'	67° 52.87'	p	s	√
NOAT161	156° 32.86'	67° 53.61'	s	p	√
NOAT172	156° 40.90'	67° 48.39'	s	p	√
NOAT225	156° 41.59'	67° 47.25'	s	-	
NOAT237	157° 56.12'	67° 42.30'	p	s	√
NOAT238	157° 56.16'	67° 42.24'	p	s	√
NOAT247	157° 51.10'	67° 40.18'	s	p	√
NOAT248	157° 51.17'	67° 40.24'	s	p	√
NOAT265	161° 05.06'	67° 56.85'	-	s	√

[1]"s" – ground control survey and photography; "p" – photography only. All slumps with fieldwork in 2010 are described in Swanson and Hill (2010)
[2]Slumps with a check (√) are shown in Fig. 1 and are described in the Results section of this report.

Most of the RTS visited in 2011 were initially photographed in 2010 and described in Swanson and Hill (2010). Eight slumps with good ground control from 2010 were simply re-photographed in 2011. Six slumps with photography only in 2010 were surveyed for ground control and re-photographed in 2011. Two slumps judged to have sub-optimal ground control in 2010 were re-surveyed and re-photographed in 2011 (GAAR008 and NOAT151). Two new slumps were surveyed and photographed in 2011: NOAT037 and NOAT265. The latter was brought to our attention by Andrew Balser (personal communication, 2010) as one of the largest and most active slumps in the Preserve. NOAT037 is largely revegetated today but is located conveniently to sample along with NOAT265; it was sampled for baseline data should it become more active in the future, but no analysis was completed at this time due to time constraints.

Eight of the slumps listed in Table 1 were photographed in 2010 (including 5 with ground survey) but not re-photographed in 2011. Some of these (NOAT004, 071, 072, 073, and 225) were judged to have low priority and skipped in 2011 to save field costs and analyst time. Slumps NOAT039, 042 were skipped due to their distance from our helibases, but were covered by imagery from another project (see below).

Ground Survey and Photography

We accessed sites by helicopter and surveyed ground control points around the perimeter of the feature using a Topcon 235W total station. This instrument provides sub-centimeter accuracy in location (including elevation) relative to the survey instrument. Five to 11 ground control points were surveyed, depending on the size of the slump. Each point was marked with an aerial marker, as was the station location, for a total of 6 to 12 control points. The absolute location of the total station was determined using recreational-grade GPS, for an accuracy of about 5 m.

With the aerial markers in place, oblique aerial photographs were shot out the door of a Robinson R44 helicopter using a Nikon D700 camera, which has a "full-frame" (35 mm) sensor, and a 50 mm lens. Photos were shot on multiple linear passes over the RTS; passes were oriented to completely cover the RTS and surrounding undisturbed ground, and to provide detail of vertical faces with various orientations. Consecutive photos overlap to provide stereo coverage of the entire slump and adjacent areas; stereo coverage is needed to produce three-dimensional models.

Oblique aerial photographs were not taken of slumps NOAT039 and NOAT042 in 2011, but 25 cm resolution vertical aerial photographs of these slumps were taken by Matt Nolan of University of Alaska for another project with NPS. These photographs were used for two-dimensional analysis of slump scarp migration as described below.

The sediments exposed in the main scarp were examined and photographed after the ground survey. Massive ground ice bodies were identified according to origin as follows. *Glacial ice* bodies are laterally extensive (not interrupted in the horizontal direction by mineral sediment, though they could be obscured by slump material); they contain coarse (> 2 mm, gravel and cobbles) and fine (< 2 mm) mineral debris; they have a smooth, horizontal upper contact with mineral sediment and no visible lower contact; and, in some cases, they display stratification of included mineral material that was flat or gently curved, oriented horizontally or with low oblique angle (Murton et al. 2005). See slumps NOAT069, -070, -074, and -237 in the Results section for good examples of glacial ice. *Pleistocene wedge ice* bodies have lateral dimensions of meters to tens of meters between vertical interruptions by mineral sediment; they are dark colored due to fine mineral material but contain no coarse (> 2 mm) material; they have a smooth, horizontal upper contact with mineral material and strongly undulating lower contact (Kanevskiy et al. 2011). See slump NOAT148 in the Results section for a good example of wedge ice.

Model Construction and Data Analysis

Three-dimensional models of RTS were constructed from oblique aerial photographs using Topcon Image Master software (www.topconpositioning.com). Each 3-D model presented here was constructed from multiple overlapping photos taken during a single flight pass.

For photo passes with ground control, common points identifiable on pairs of adjacent photos (known as "pass points") and the aerial markers with known coordinates (ground control points) were located on the photos. Image Master used these points to determine the location and orientation of the camera when each photo was taken, and to compute the locations of the pass points (in units of meters relative to the survey instrument location). The computation of camera and pass point locations was by bundle adjustment, which means that all photos, pass points, and ground control points were used simultaneously to compute the optimal solution.

For photo passes without ground control survey, ground control was obtained from a model created in the year with ground control. To accomplish this, distinctive landmarks ("tie points"), typically rocks or small clumps of vegetation, were located on photos from both years. About 15 tie points were established per slump. The tie points were marked on photos from the year with ground control as described above; the absolute location in meters relative to the survey station was computed for the points by bundle adjustment. The same landmarks were marked on the photographs from the year without ground control; then the coordinates for these points (obtained from the bundle adjustment of the survey year) were input as ground control for the bundle adjustment of the un-surveyed year. The result is two models that are co-registered and have dimensions determined by the survey year.

It is often difficult to locate common landmarks among subtle natural features on photographs taken in different years from different perspectives, but this is necessary to transfer ground control to photos from un-surveyed years as described above. To facilitate location of these common landmarks ("tie points"), two photos of the same general area from the different years were loaded into ArcMap and processed using the Georeferencing tool. This tool allows one to locate common landmarks between two images and progressively rotates, scales, and warps one of the images to match the other as landmarks are identified. As the two images align it becomes possible to confidently find common landmarks between the photos, and ArcMap can produce a table of coordinates of these landmarks on both photos that can be imported into Image Master. The ArcMap georeferencing tool was used in this case only to aid in locating landmarks to enter into Image Master as tie points between two photos from different years (as described in the previous paragraph). Thus the specific type of georeferencing transformation used and the accuracy obtained are not crucial.

After bundle adjustment, a three-dimensional surface of each slump was constructed in Image Master using a grid spacing of 2 m. This model was used to create orthophotographs and cross-sectional diagrams, and to calculate slump area, main scarp height, slope, and volume change. (An orthophotograph has a vertical perspective, and all distortions due to perspective and elevation removed, like a map.) To calculate change in slump area and rate of main scarp migration, the trace of the main scarp was drawn along the uppermost large extensional fracture if an obvious vertical face was not present.

5

To save analyst time, I developed an abbreviated process that is adequate for two-dimensional (2-D) registration of models and computation of changes in area and rate of main scarp migration (but not volume). For the 2-D registration process, a model was created for the year without ground control using pass points only. The result was a 3-D model with unknown scale and orientation. An approximately vertical orthophotograph of the slump was created from this model, imported into ArcMap, and georeferenced onto a true vertical orthophotograph from the year with ground control. This abbreviated process was used for several slumps that changed little between the two photo dates (slumps NOAT161, 247, and 248), on slump NOAT151 (where 3-D model construction was difficult from 2010 photographs), and on slump NOAT069 (where ground control in 2010 was not well positioned).

Two slumps had a ground-controlled 3-D model in 2010 and vertical aerial photographs from 2011 (NOAT039 and 042). Simple spline georeferencing of one vertical aerial photograph of each slump to the respective 2010 model was adequate for 2-D analysis of scarp migration.

The camera location and accuracy parameters reported in this report are described below. The average for each parameter was computed for the set of all photos used in the model.

> Camera angle φ, in degrees from vertical
> Base:height ratio – the ratio between the distance traveled between photos and the distance to target. Wider ratios (greater than 0.2) provide better elevational accuracy, but result in slivers between photos without overlap, and thus without topography, in the foreground
> Control point error in x, m – the root mean square error of the computed location of the ground control points (by the bundle adjustment) in the x direction (east-west) relative to their actual location as determined by ground survey.
> Control point error in y, m – as above, except the error is in the y direction (north-south)
> Control point error in z, m – as above, except the error is in the elevation.

Orthophotographs of the slumps in the figures in this report are all oriented so that the main scarp of the slump is on the left side of the figure and downslope is to the right. A north arrow is provided to indicate cardinal orientation.

Results

Slump activity varied greatly. Main scarp migration between 2010 and 2011 ranged from just a few meters in slumps NOAT247 and NOAT248 to over 50 m in slump NOAT069 (Table 2). The change in slump area ranged from negligible in slumps NOAT247 and NOAT248 to about 1 ha (10,000 m^2) in NOAT 070.

Table 2. Summary of slump characteristics

Slump	Main scarp retreat, m	Main scarp height, m	Scarp migr- ation mode[1]	Slump area in 2011, m^2	Area increase, 2010-2011, m^2	Mean subsidence in new slump area, m	Volume loss in upper subsidence zone, m^3	Volume increase in upper accumulation zone, m^3
GAAR008	25-30	2	f	12,713	1,919	1.3	3,443	310
NOAT039[2]	1-20	10	f	48,816	3,669	-	-	-
NOAT042	10-15	10	f	18,712	2,556	-	-	-
NOAT068	20-40	5	f	28,025	6,986	2.0	15,008	8,123
NOAT069	50-65	1.5	f	15,541	4,784	-	-	-
NOAT070	25-45	4	f	45,884	10,063	2.9	36,135	9,616
NOAT074	20-35	3	f	17,161	4,078	2.0	9,710	2,419
NOAT076	15-20	4	f	10,974	1,587	1.4	3,484	2,078
NOAT148	10-15	8	f	17,920	2,792	3.3	12,916	1,221
NOAT151	20-35	5	m	49,861	6,141	-	-	-
NOAT159	5-18	3	e	7,601	1,118	1.8	3,376	454
NOAT160	5-10	2	e	11,827	984	1.1	2,138	78
NOAT161	1-25	2	m	15,578	1,737	-	-	-
NOAT172	10-12	10	f	19,485	1,731	3.0	8,079	1,494
NOAT237	25-35	4	f	12,561	3,752	2.3	10,627	2,489
NOAT238	10-20	4	f	5,265	601	1.5	1,444	527
NOAT247	1-5	5	e	7,923	324	-	-	-
NOAT248	0-5	4	e	9,498	271	-	-	-
NOAT265[3]	-	20	f	30,241	-	-	-	-

[1]Predominant mode of main scarp migration (see Fig. 2): e – extensional flow, f – fall and flow, m – mixed (both extensional and fall and flow).
[2]Data are missing in the final 3 columns for NOAT039, -042, -069, -151, -161, -247, and -248 because only 2-dimensional change analyses were completed (see Methods, Model Construction and Data Analysis).
[3]Slump NOAT265 lacks change data because it has only one year of data (2011).

The most rapid rates of main scarp migration occurred in slumps with a vertical main scarp that exposed a relatively thin overburden layer (1.5 to 2 m) over a continuous layer of glacial ice (see the escarpment photos in the sections below on slumps NOAT068, 069, 070, and 074). These scarps migrated 20 to 65 m during the approximately 13 months between the sample dates. Scarp migration in these slumps was by a mechanism referred to here as "fall and flow": material fell off the vertical main scarp, slid down the exposed ice into a zone of liquefied mud just below, where it continued to flow downhill (Fig. 2). Turf blocks and clumps of vegetation usually disintegrated or sank, and the liquefied zone was nearly pure gray mud that gradually de-watered and became more solid downslope from the scarp. The liquefied mud zone would not support our weight and hindered our approach to the scarp.

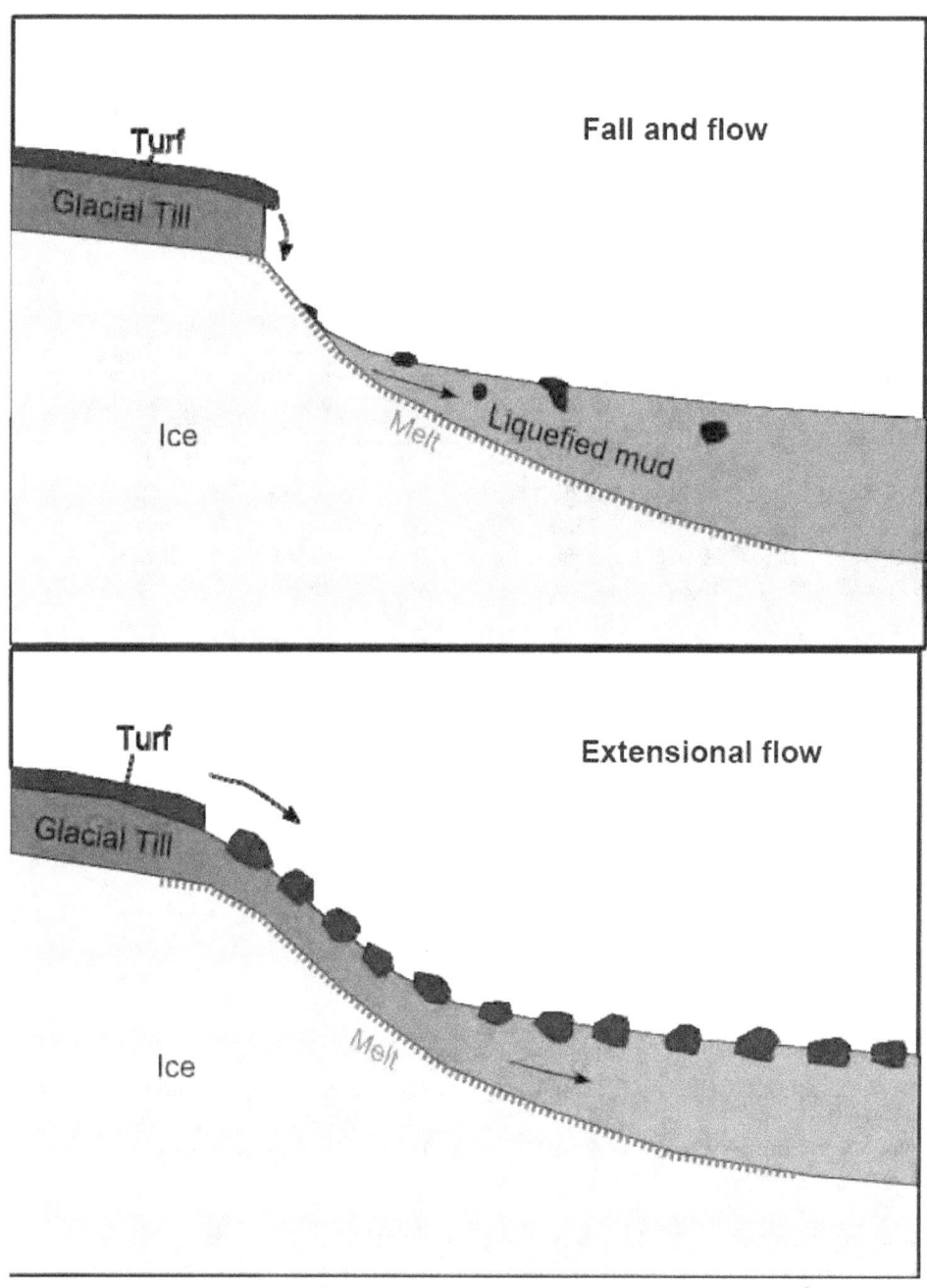

Figure 2. Cross-sectional diagrams of escarpment forms in retrogressive thaw slumps. *Fall and flow* escarpments (upper) consist of a turf surface layer (including moss, organic soil horizons and upper mineral horizons strongly bound by plant roots) over a near-vertical face in glacial till (usually 1.5 to 2 m high). Below the till, the scarp exposes a sloping ice surface. Material falls down the scarp, slides down the ice, and forms a mass of liquefied mud that flows downhill. Most turf blocks fall apart or sink in the mud. Melt of the underlying ice presumably continues downslope of the scarp until the overburden is sufficiently thick to insulate it from summer thaw. *Extensional flow* escarpments (lower) are rounded and do not expose ice. The turf is split into elongate blocks (fractures occur parallel to the slope, so the long dimension of the blocks runs into the page on the diagram) at the convex point of the slope. Breaching of the turf layer and thinning of the till allow melt of the underlying ice, which continues downslope until a sufficient insulating layers forms again. Water released by thaw of the underlying ice body and lesser amounts of ice within the till are sufficient to allow flow but do not produce as fluid a mass as in the fall and flow scarps.

Slumps with very tall main scarps (NOAT039, 042, 148, and 172) exposed thicker sediment layers and showed slower rates of scarp migration, generally about 10 m. These slumps are on older moraines that pre-date the last glacial maximum and have large Pleistocene ice wedges. Their mode of migration was by the "fall and flow" mechanism, though the thickness of the overburden relative to the ice was greater than in the slumps described in the previous paragraph. Exposures of glacial ice were observed at the base of the scarp in most of these slumps, but this layer was frequently obscured by slump debris and did not form an obvious, continuous layer.

Some slump scarps migrated by a mechanism referred to here as "extensional flow" (see Fig. 2 and the sections below on slumps NOAT159, 160, 161, 247, and 248). No ice was exposed in these scarps (though its presence could often be inferred based on nearby exposures) and the escarpments were more gradual. Elongate blocks of turf were separated by long fractures along the slope contour. These blocks typically survived their trip down the scarp and were preserved on the slump floor below. We could approach the scarp without difficulty in these slumps by walking on the turf blocks. Liquefied mud was typically present between the turf blocks near the main scarp, but its area was much less than in the fall and flow slumps. Main scarps migrated by the extensional flow mechanism less than 20 m between the two years, and in some cases only a few meters.

Most of the subsidence in both slump types occurred in the new portion, between the positions of the 2010 and 2011 main scarps (Figs. 3 and 4). The main subsidence area generally coincided with the area of liquefied mud present just below the main scarp in the second year. The amount of subsidence was minimal in inactive slumps and ranged up to over 30,000 cubic meters in the most active slump (Table 2). The active slumps also had an accumulation zone, below the subsidence zone, where the surface elevation rose, typically 1 to 2 m (Figs. 3 and 4). The volume of subsidence in most slumps was several times as great as the volume increase in the accumulation zone (Table 2). This accumulation zone typically began within 10 m of subsidence zone (i.e., near the location of the base of the previous year's scarp) and extended up to 50 m downslope. The accumulation zone coincided with the firmer ground just below the liquefied mud zone. Bulging and fracturing of the surface in this firmer area suggested that it acted as a dam that holds back the liquefied mud while deforming. Landmarks below the accumulation zone appeared stable, with the exception of some vegetation growth and minor changes in small runoff channels.

Camera angles (Table 3) were slightly more vertical in 2011 than 2010 (when most were about 60°; Swanson and Hill 2010), as a result of an effort in 2011 to make photos as vertical as possible without the landing gear appearing in the photo. Base:height ratios (Table 3) were lower in 2011 (near 0.1) than 2010 (when they were mostly 0.15 and 0.20; Swanson and Hill 2010). This resulted from a conscious effort to shoot photographs with more overlap in 2011, because of problems with insufficient overlap in 2010. For single stereo pairs, the accuracy of measurements decreases with smaller base:height ratios, so there is a trade-off. However, the bundle adjustment process (which combines all the photo pairs into one model) appears to compensate for low base:height ratios with redundancy in computations using multiple photos of the same points. As a test I added alternate photos to several models as stereo pairs (which doubled the base:height ratio) and obtained no improvement in bundle adjustment accuracy.

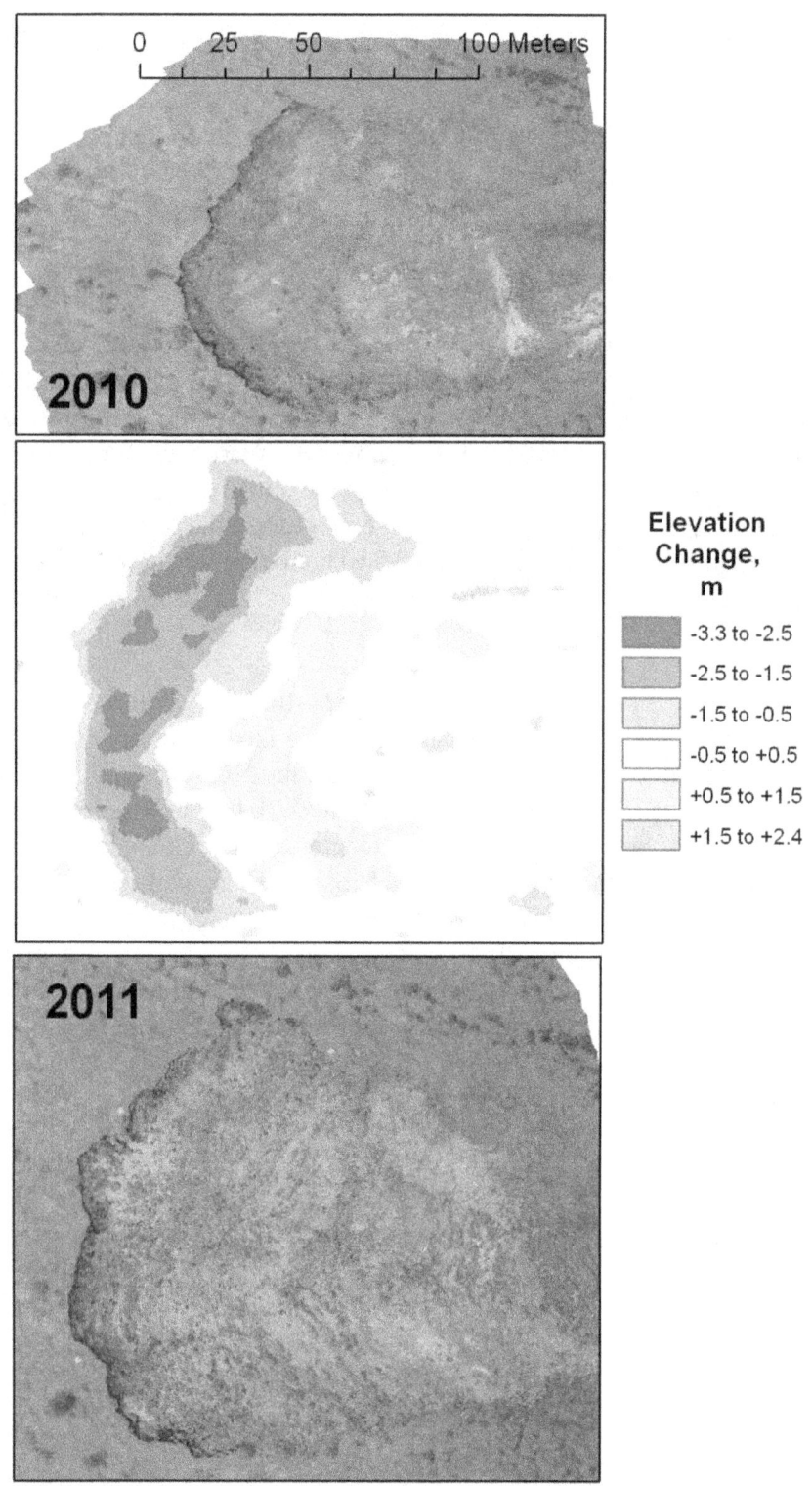

Figure 3. Elevation change between 2010 and 2011 in an example thaw slump (NOAT074). The slump grew uphill to the left. Subsidence of up to several meters occurred in the new part of the slump, while the surface rose up to 2.4 m in a band just below.

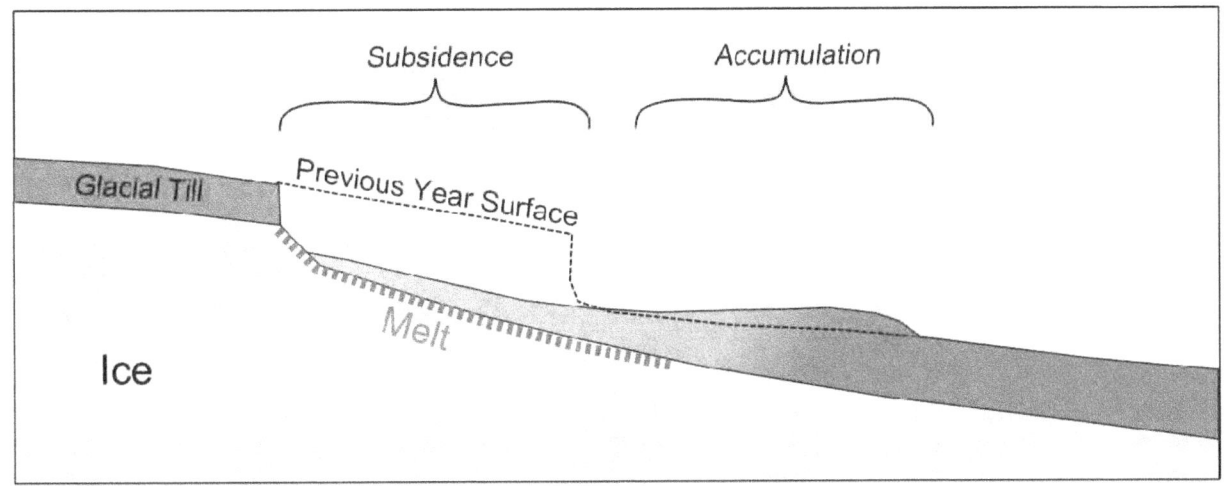

Figure 4. Diagram of thaw slump subsidence and accumulation zones. Most of the subsidence occurs between the current-year and previous-year escarpments. Accumulation occurs just downslope where the liquefied mud (high water content shown in light brown) flows downhill and builds up behind the more rigid, de-watered sediment further downslope (sediment with low water content is shown in dark brown). Melt of the underlying ice occurs where the mineral overburden is too thin to accommodate the entire seasonal depth of thaw.

Table 3. Camera parameters summary for 2011 photos with 3-D models

Slump	Pass	Mean camera view angle ω, ° from vertical	Base:height ratio
GAAR008	2011B	37	0.13
NOAT068	2011B	45	0.09
NOAT070	2011A	54	0.08
NOAT074	2011F	55	0.08
NOAT148	2011A	51	0.11
NOAT151	2011F	46	0.09
NOAT159	2011E	46	0.09
NOAT160	2011E	48	0.08
NOAT172	2011A	48	0.11
NOAT237 and 238	2011D	60	0.10
NOAT265	2011F	58	0.09

Mean control point error and tie point errors (Table 4) provide minimum estimates of error in the 3-D models. Control point error is the difference between the input control point coordinates and the computed coordinates for these points in the model. Tie point error is the difference between the input coordinates for landmarks taken from the surveyed model and the computed locations for these landmarks in the un-surveyed model. Generally the tie point errors in the un-surveyed models were similar to or somewhat larger than the control point errors in the models from which they were tied. All are less than 30 cm for all three coordinates, except for the un-surveyed 2011 model of NOAT070. Control and tie point errors are larger in models of larger area (e.g., NOAT070).

Table 4. Model accuracy summary

Slump	Pass	Surveyed Model Mean control point error, m			Pass	Unsurveyed Model Mean tie point error, m		
		x	y	z		x	y	z
GAAR008	2011B	0.0485	0.0577	0.0254	2010B	0.0882	0.0824	0.1060
NOAT068	2010C	0.0766	0.0784	0.0705	2011B	0.0667	0.0624	0.0465
NOAT070	2010A	0.0240	0.0372	0.0376	2011A	1.7764	0.8765	0.6796
NOAT074	2011F	0.0843	0.0567	0.0627	2010A	0.0224	0.0223	0.0342
NOAT076	2011A	0.0368	0.0486	0.0340	2010A	0.2350	0.2892	0.2248
NOAT148	2010B	0.1005	0.0514	0.0908	2011A	0.1316	0.1245	0.1071
NOAT151	2011F	0.1406	0.1646	0.0945	-	-	-	-
NOAT159	2011E	0.0313	0.0331	0.0296	2010A	0.0269	0.0642	0.0475
NOAT160	2011E	0.0305	0.0346	0.0375	2010A	0.0431	0.0535	0.0555
NOAT161	2010A	0.0126	0.0298	0.0177	-	-	-	-
NOAT172	2010B	0.0175	0.0538	0.0228	2011A	0.0356	0.0324	0.0346
NOAT237 and 238	2011D	0.2785	0.2992	0.2025	2010A	0.0493	0.0541	0.0856
NOAT247 and 248	2010A	0.0280	0.0776	0.0383				
NOAT265	2011F	0.2561	0.1742	0.1577	-	-	-	-

GAAR008

The main scarp of GAAR008 advanced rapidly (up to 30 m) between 25 June 2010 and 20 July 2011 (Fig. 5), increasing in area by about 1920 m^2 (0.192 ha). The main scarp (Fig. 6) was still about 2 m high at its highest point, but in 2011 buried glacial ice was not visible in the main scarp as it was in 2010, suggesting that the main scarp retreat may slow down in the future.

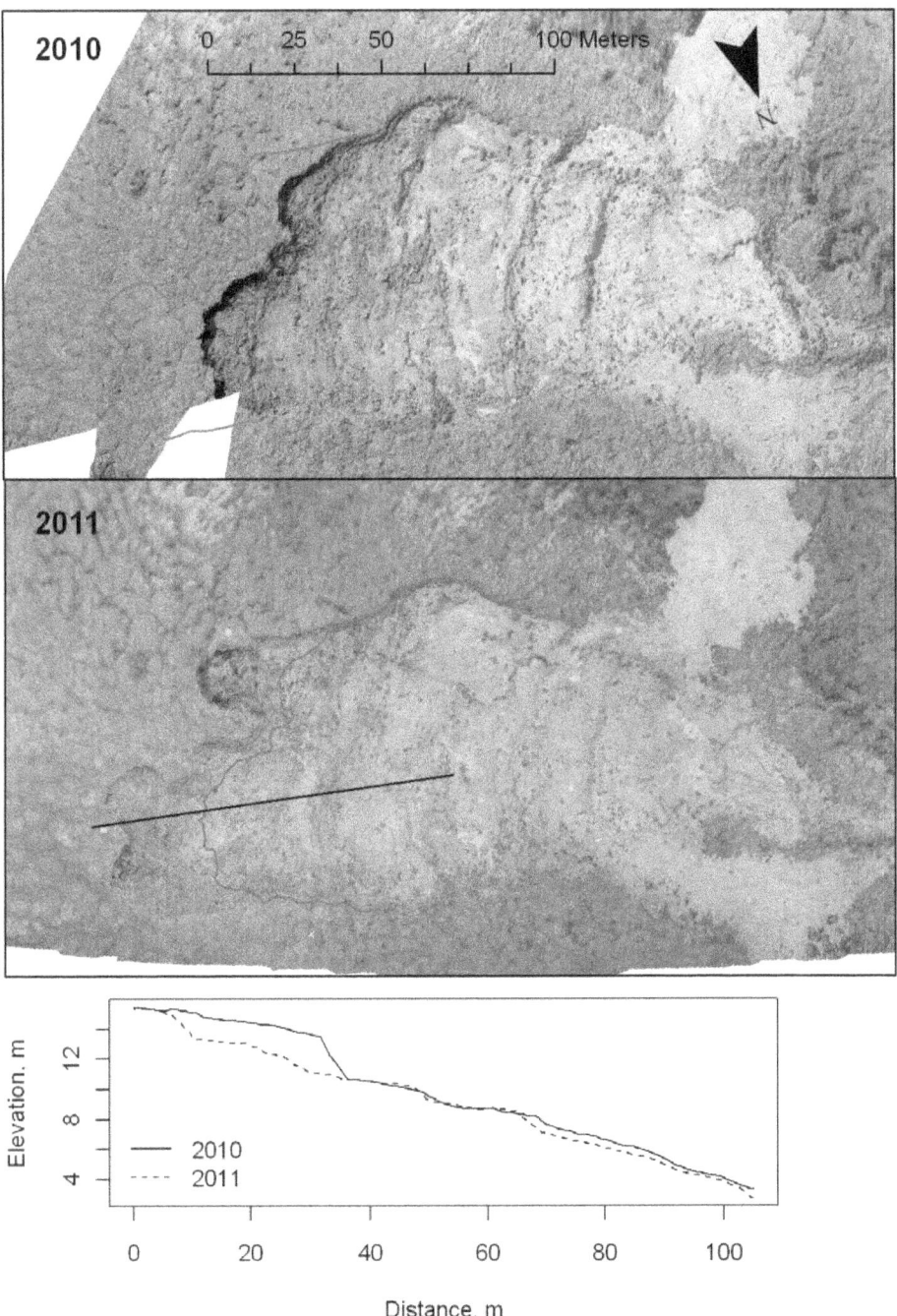

Figure 5. Orthophotographs of slump GAAR008 on 25 June 2010 (upper) and 20 July 2011 (lower) with cross-sectional diagram (below). Here and in all subsequent figures, the red lines show the location of the main scarp in the other year on each photo, and the thin black line on the lower photo is the location of the cross-section.

Figure 6. Main scarp of GAAR008 in 2011. The main scarp was still active and about 2 m high, but in contrast to 2010, buried glacial was not widely exposed below the glacial till.

NOAT039

NOAT039 is a spectacular large slump with 10-m main scarp exposing large Pleistocene ice wedges and glacial ice (Swanson and Hill 2010). It showed interesting variability in growth rate along the length of the main scarp between the photo dates of 24 June 2010 and 25 Sept 2011 (Fig. 7). The fastest scarp migration (up to 20 m) occurred in the northern part, where the scarp was indistinct and migrated by extensional flow. The vertical portions of the scarp, which are on the southwest side and face northeast, migrated more slowly (1 to 10 m) but remained vertical.

Figure 7. Orthophotograph (24 June 2010; left) and georeferenced vertical aerial photograph (25 Sept 2011; right) of slump NOAT039. (2011 photo by Matt Nolan, University of Alaska Fairbanks.)

NOAT042

NOAT042, like its larger neighbor NOAT039, had a tall main scarp with Pleistocene ice wedges exposed (Swanson and Hill 2010). The north-facing scarp migrated a moderate distance (10-15 m) between 24 June 2010 and 25 September 2011, and maintained verticality throughout its length (Fig. 8). Depositional features and vegetation on the scarp floor showed little change.

Figure 8. Orthophotograph (24 June 2010; left) and georeferenced vertical aerial photograph (25 Sept 2011; right) of slump NOAT042. (2011 photo by Matt Nolan, University of Alaska Fairbanks).

NOAT068

NOAT 068 experienced rapid main scarp retreat of 20 to 40 m between 22 June 2010 and 19 July 2011 (Fig. 9). Judging from the cross-section, the main scarp was about 4 m high, and a distinct line separating the upper glacial till from the lower debris-rich glacial ice was readily visible on the aerial photographs (Fig. 10). NOAT068 showed a distinct zone of accumulation of material just below the subsidence zone (see the cross-section in Fig. 9). The lower half of the slump showed little change from 2010.

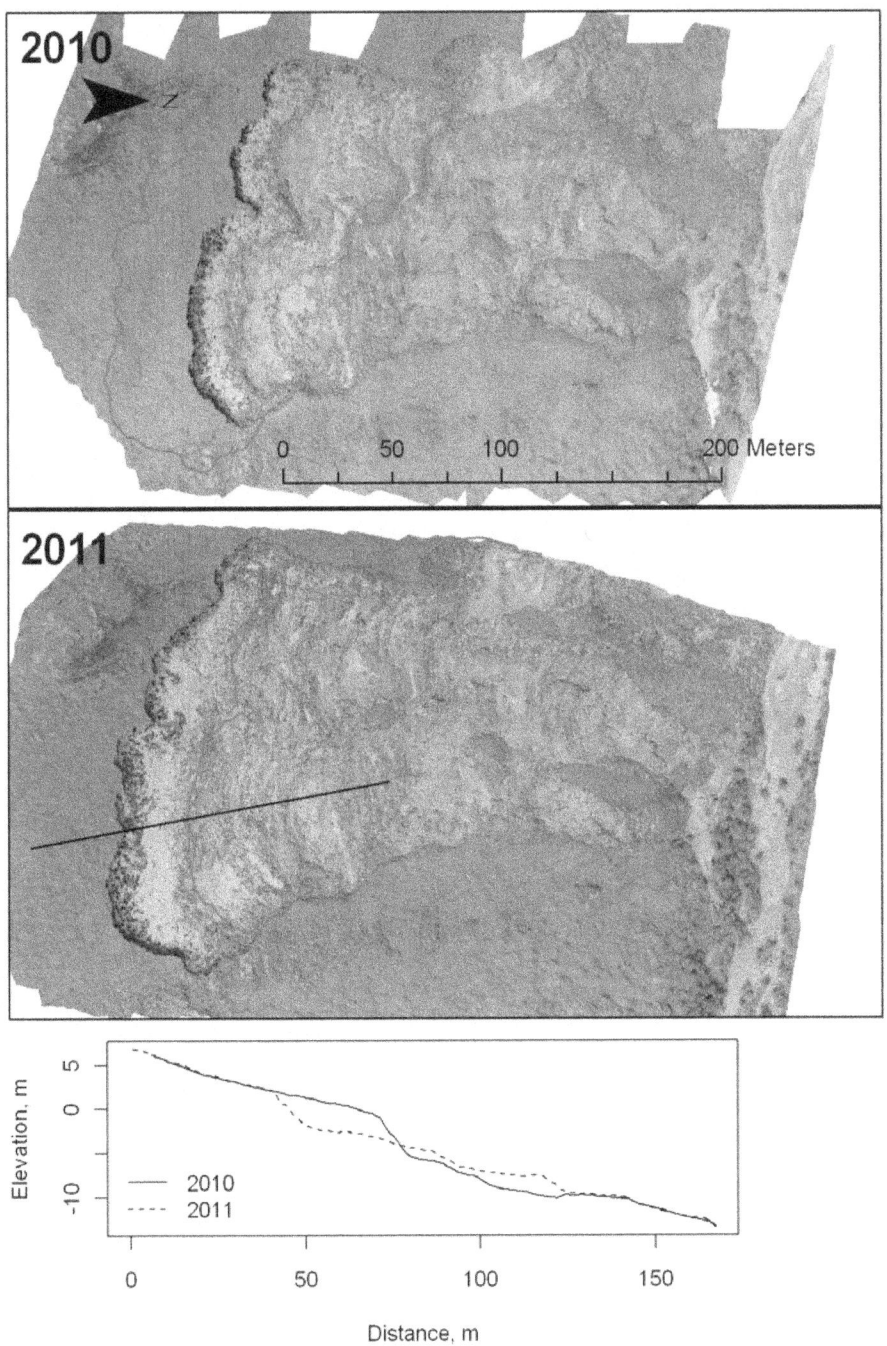

Figure 9. Orthophotographs and cross-sections of slump NOAT068 on 22 June 2010 (upper) and 19 July 2011 (lower).

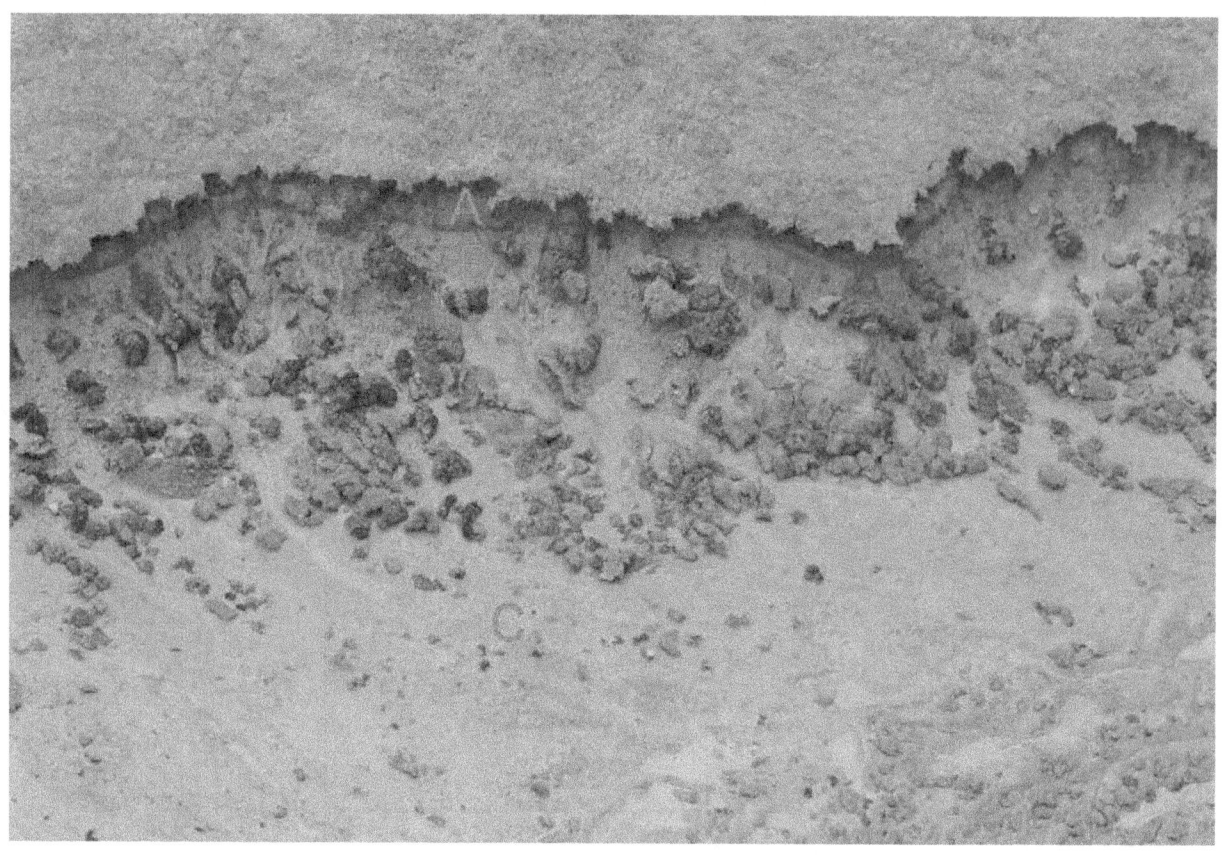

Figure 10. Oblique aerial photograph of the main scarp of slump NOAT068 in 2011. The main scarp was about 4 m high and had the main features observed in 2010 of a glacial till surface layer (A) over a sloping face of debris-rich glacial ice (B), with a zone of liquefied mud just below (C). Intact pieces of turf are seen sliding down the ice slope in the liquefied zone.

NOAT069

NOAT069 had very rapid main scarp retreat, over 60 m at the apex, allowing this rather narrow slump (just 75 m wide) to grow by nearly half a hectare between 22 June 2010 and 19 July 2011(Fig. 11). Volume data are not presented here for this slump because the survey used for ground control (completed in 2010) surrounds the adjacent slump NOAT068 and is not well positioned for detailed elevational control of NOAT069. However, the 2-dimensional control is adequate for distance and area measurements of NOAT069. The geologic materials and ground ice exposed in the scarp of NOAT069 (Fig. 12) are similar to other slumps in the vicinity (e.g., NOAT068 and NOAT070).

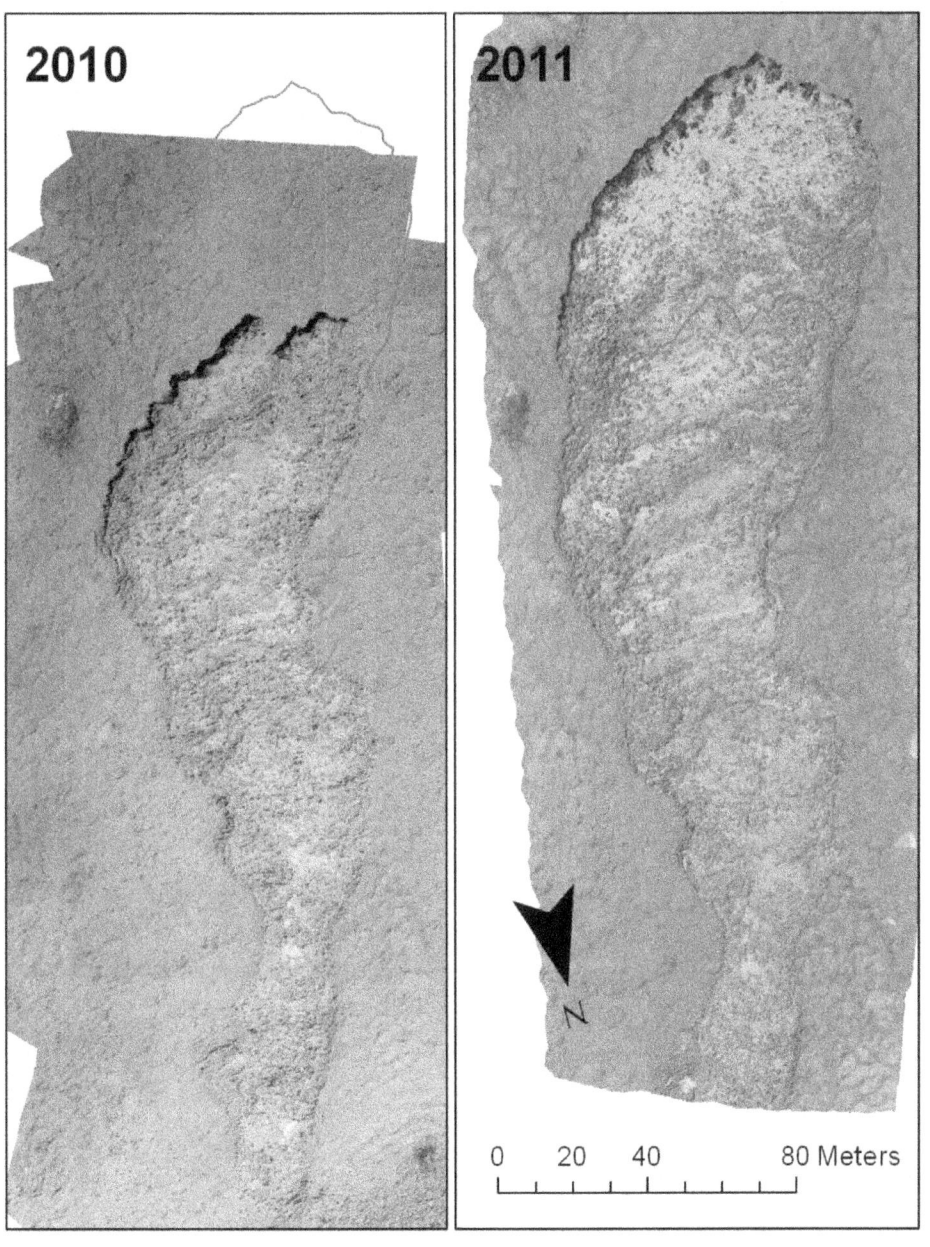

Figure 11. Orthophotographs of slump NOAT069 on 22 June 2010 (left) and 19 July 2011 (right).

Figure 12. Oblique aerial photograph of the main scarp of slump NOAT069 in 2011. Surface till sediment forms a nearly vertical face (A) over glacial ice that forms a sloping surface (B) leading down to a zone of liquefied mud (C). Freshly fallen sediment (D) slides down the ice and is incorporated into the mud. Note the foliation in the glacial ice just to the right of (D). The scarp height is estimated at about 4 m.

NOAT070

NOAT070 was very active between the photos dates of 22 June 2010 and 19 July 2011. The slump grew in area by 10,060 m^2 (approximately 1 ha) as the main scarp retreated 25 to 45 m (Fig. 13). The mean subsidence depth in the newly slumped area was 2.9 m, and the estimated total volume of subsidence between these two dates was about 36,000 m^3. Just below the main area of subsidence there was a zone of accumulation (see the cross-section, Fig. 13). The estimated volume of material added here was 9,319 m^3 over an area of 9,616 m^2 area for an average increase of about 1 m; the maximum rise was 1.5 to 2 m. Thus the subsidence exceeded accumulation by nearly four-fold. There is no evidence for major transport of material down the slump below the immediate areas of loss and accumulation near the main scarp: the lower two-thirds of the slump appeared essentially unchanged between the photo dates. The main scarp exposed a relatively thin layer of glacial till over glacial ice (Fig. 14).

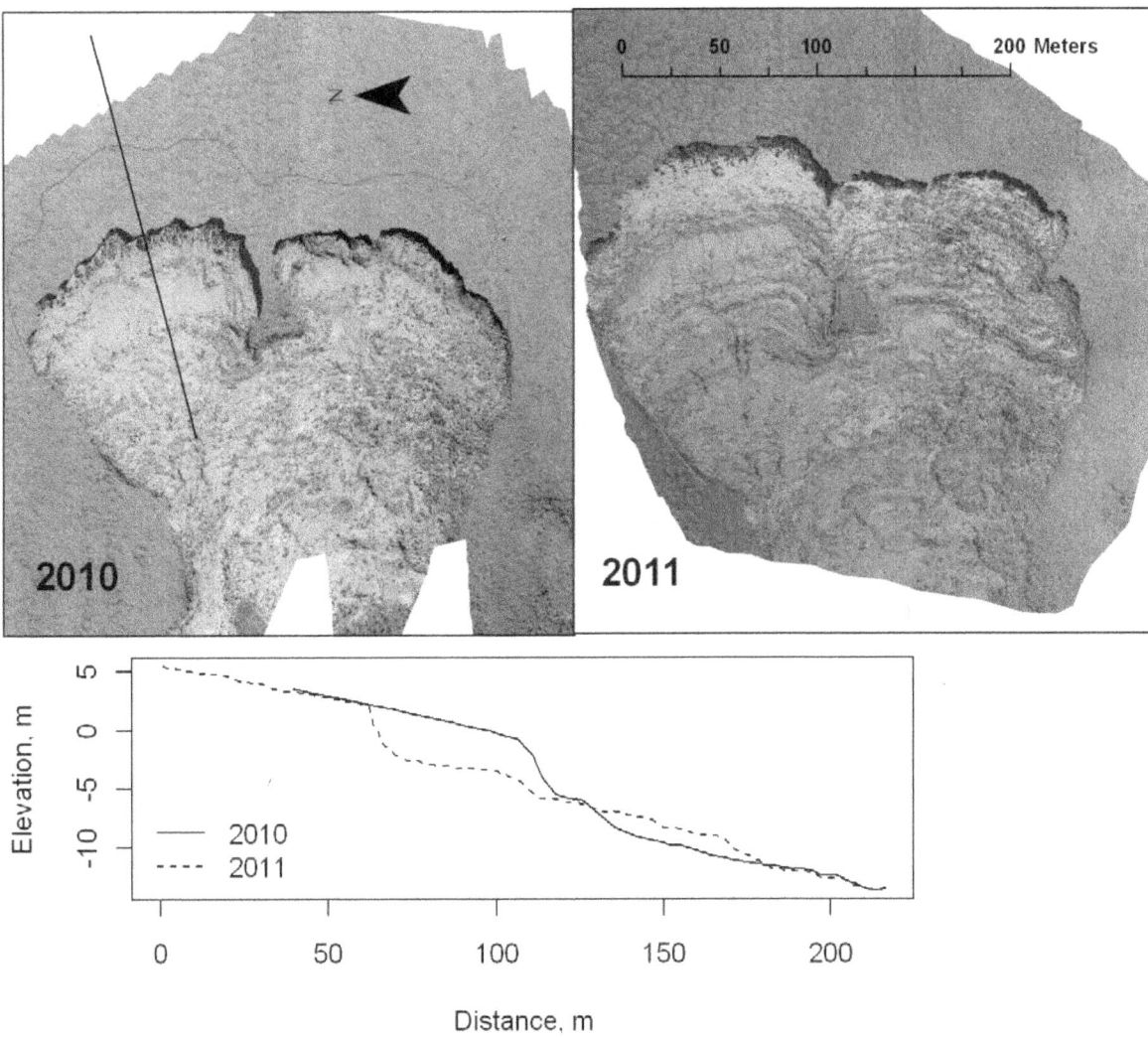

Figure 13. Orthophotographs of slump NOAT070 on 22 June 2010 (left) and 19 July 2011 (right) with cross sectional diagram (below).

21

Figure 14. Oblique aerial photograph of the main scarp of NOAT070 in 2011. The scarp is 4-5 m high and exposes glacial till forming a vertical face (A) over sloping debris-rich glacial ice with foliation visible (B), leading down to a zone of liquefied mud (C).

NOAT074

NOAT074 showed rapid growth between the photos dates of 25 June 2010 and 19 July 2011, with 20 to 35 m of scarp migration (Fig. 15). The main scarp (Fig. 16) was about 3 m high and exposed glacial till over glacial ice, like other slumps in this vicinity. The volume of material lost in the newly subsided area (9,710 m^3) greatly exceeded the accumulation just below (2,419 m^3), while the lower half of the slump had stable topography and surface features (Fig. 15).

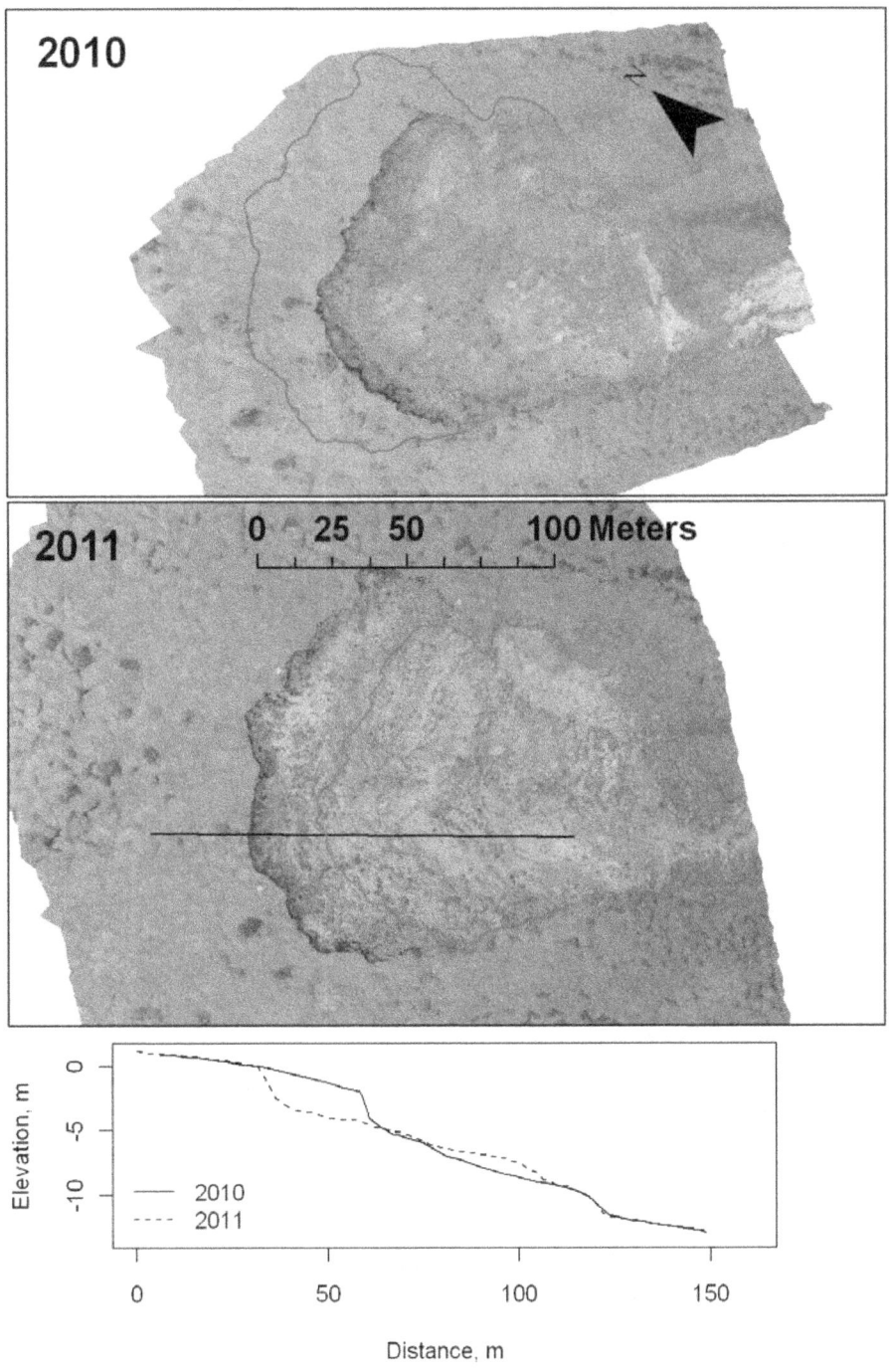

Figure 15. Orthophotographs and cross-sections of slump NOAT074 on 25 June 2010 (upper) and 19 July 2011 (lower).

Figure 16. Main scarp of slump NOAT074 in 2011. About 1.75 m of glacial till (A) forms a vertical face over debris-rich glacial ice (B) that slopes down to liquefied mud (C).

NOAT076

NOAT076 showed moderate growth, with 15-20 m of main scarp migration between 25 June 2010 and 19 July 2011 (Fig. 17). The main scarp was about 2.5 m high, with basal glacial ice exposed only in a small section of the main scarp (Fig. 18). This slump had grown to near the top of the local slope, which should impede future growth. In this slump the volume of accumulated material was over half of the total volume of subsidence, the largest proportion of accumulation in any slump in the study.

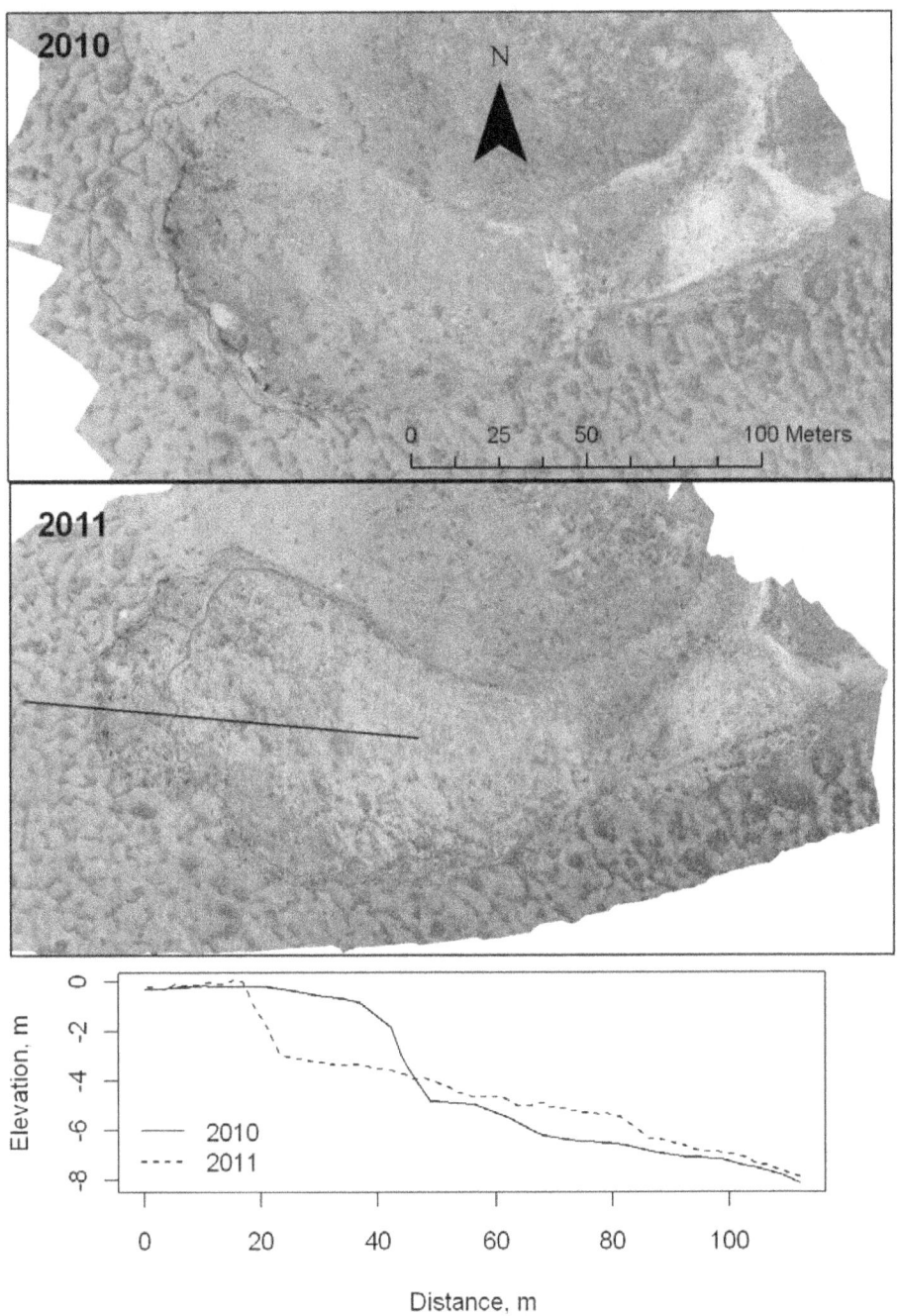

Figure 17. Orthophotographs and cross-sections of slump NOAT076 on 25 June 2010 (upper) and 19 July 2011 (lower).

Figure 18. Main scarp of slump NOAT076 in 2011. Glacial till with increasing pebble and cobble content near the base (A) overlies debris-rich basal glacial ice (B). Along most of the scarp, slumped glacial till (presumably obscuring glacial ice) is present below a short vertical face (C).

NOAT148

NOAT148 experienced 10-15 m of scarp migration and about 0.3 ha growth in area between 23 June 2010 and 18 July 2011 (Fig. 19). As a result of its tall main scarp (up to 8 m; Swanson and Hill 2010), this modest amount of scarp retreat produced a comparatively large volume of subsidence, nearly 13,000 m^3 (Table 2). This greatly exceeded the small area of accumulation below of about 1200 m^3. The lower part of the slump changed little between the years beyond some minor increase in plant cover. The main scarp exposed large Pleistocene ice wedges (Fig. 20) and glacial ice, as it did in 2010.

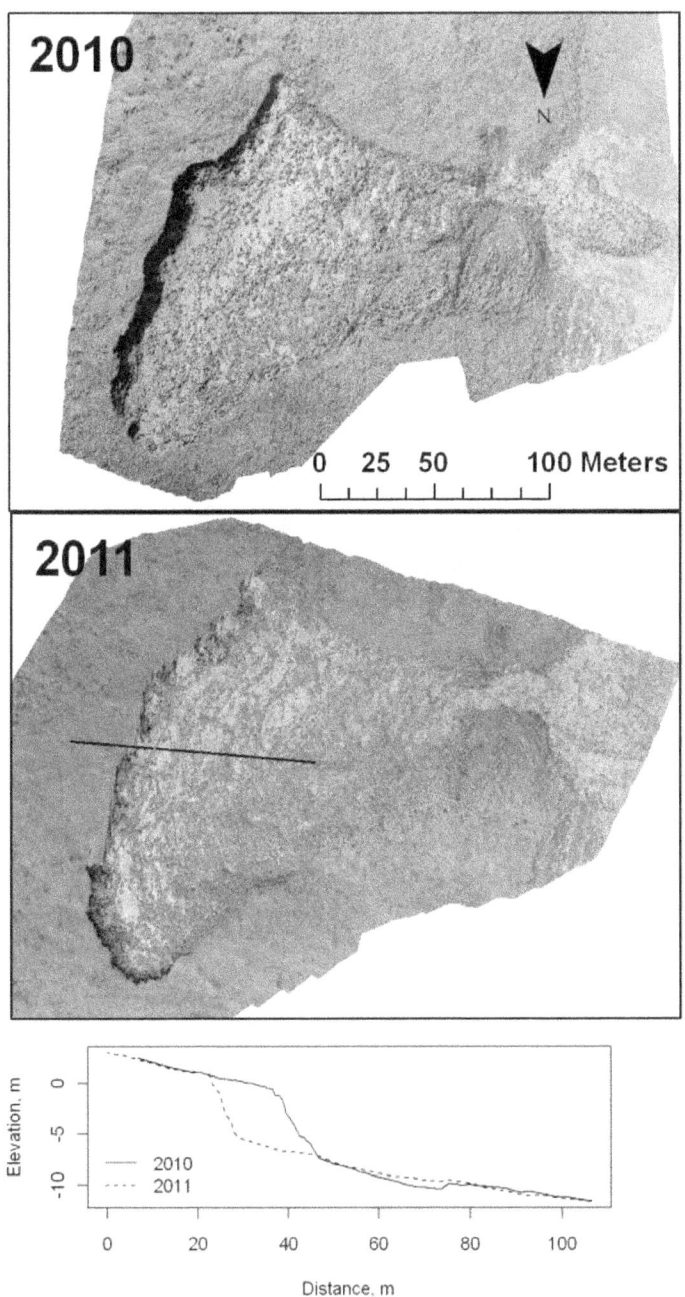

Figure 19. Orthophotographs and cross-sections of slump NOAT148 on 23 June 2010 (upper) and 18 July 2011 (lower).

Figure 20. The main scarp of slump NOAT148 in 2011 exposed large Pleistocene ice wedges.

NOAT151

NOAT151 is a large slump (over 4 ha) that added another 0.6 ha of area and 20 to 35 m of scarp migration in the high-relief, vertical (southeastern) section of the main scarp (Fig. 21). This portion of the main scarp maintained the height of 5 m noted in 2010. This slump is in older glacial till (Itkillik I; Hamilton 2010). The north half of the main scarp is advancing into an area that slumped in the 1970s (visible on a 1977 aerial photograph; see Swanson and Hill 2010) while the south half is in material that shows no signs of prior slumping. The main scarp in the previously un-slumped portion consisted of about a meter of partly oxidized loamy material with minor gravel (interpreted as eolian sediment mixed with underlying till by frost action), over about 4 m of stony glacial till that grades into debris-rich glacial ice near the bottom of the section (Fig. 22). In the previously slumped area the overburden is thinner, with a sharp contact onto basal glacial ice. In the previously slumped scarp is an exposure of a Pleistocene ice wedge that cuts the glacial ice (Fig. 23); presumably the wedge previously extended down from the overlying till but was truncated by thaw during the previous slumping event.

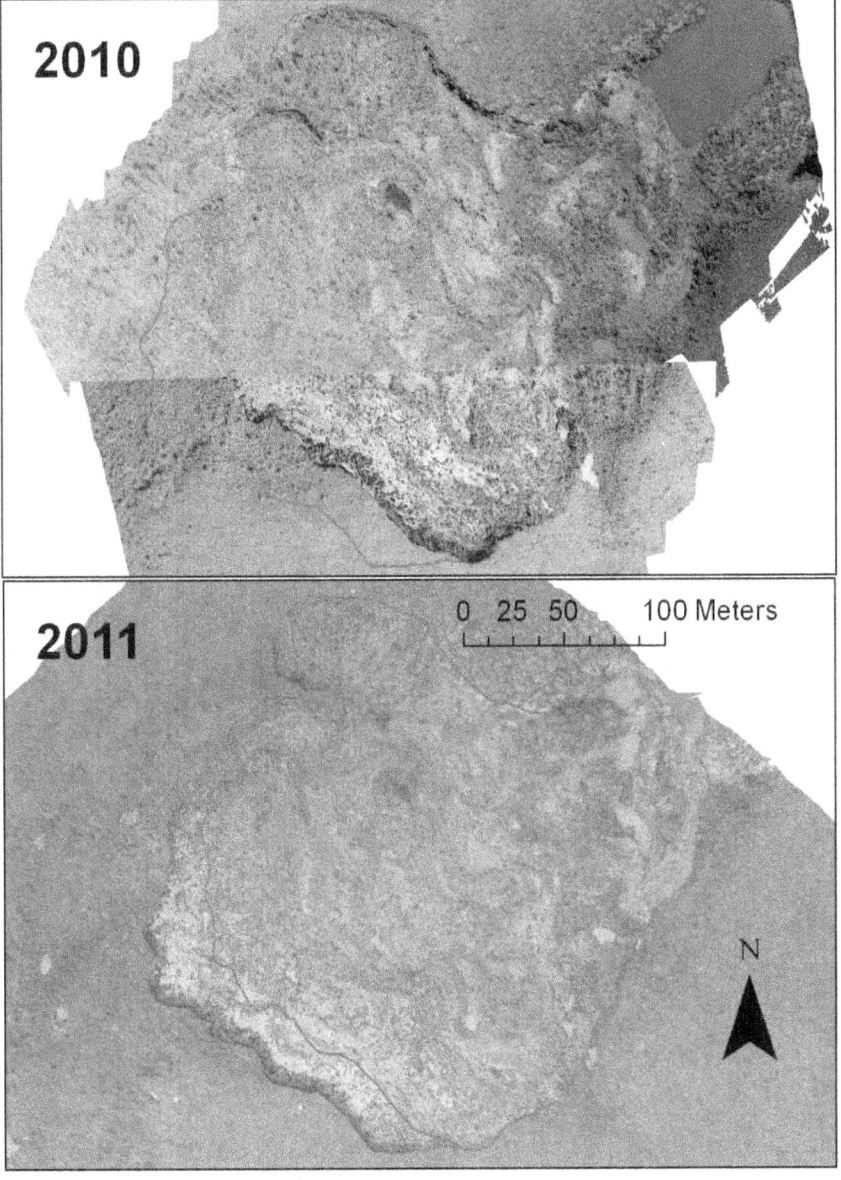

Figure 21.
Orthophotographs of slump NOAT151 in 2010 and 2011.

The northern lobe of the slump had a rounded main scarp and was slumping by extensional flow; here the migration between 2010 and 2011 was less than 15 m. NOAT151 was analyzed in two dimensions due to the difficulties encountered in obtaining and registering a good 3-D model from the 2011 photographs.

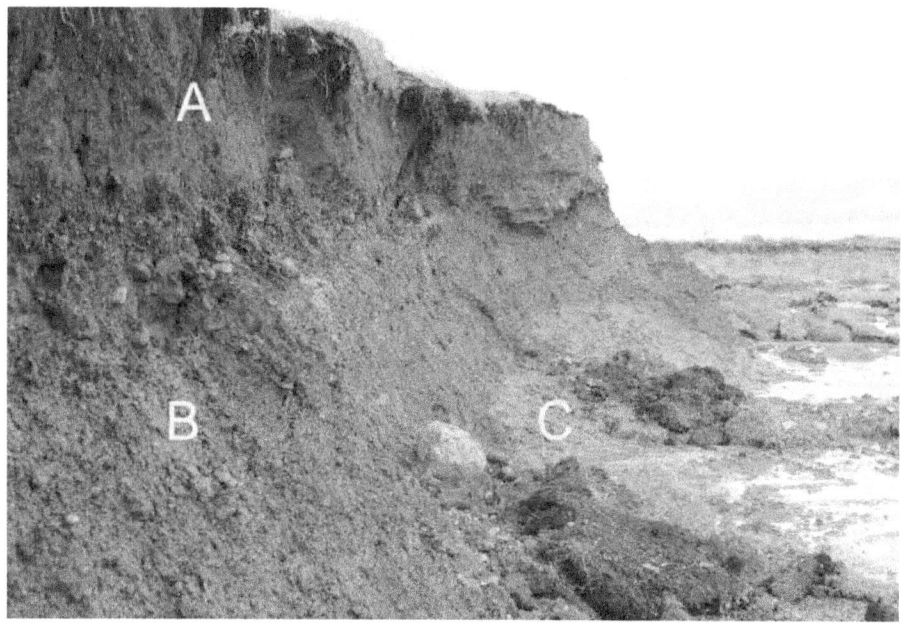

Figure 22. Main scarp of NOAT151 in the portion that did not slump in the 1970s. About 1 m of partially oxidized, loamy material (A; loess mixed slightly with underlying till by frost action) overlies about 4 m of stony glacial till (B), grading into debris-rich glacial ice near the bottom of the section (C).

Figure 23. Main scarp of NOAT151 in the portion that slumped in the 1970s. About 1.5 m of glacial till (A; reworked by slumping) overlies basal glacial ice (B). A large Pleistocene ice wedge (C) cuts into the glacial ice and was truncated by thaw at the top of the glacial ice during the previous slumping episode.

NOAT159

Slump NOAT159 had a moderate rate of main scarp migration between the two years (5-18 m, Fig. 24). The main scarp was not highly active in 2011, as shown by the lack of exposed ice or a liquefied mud zone (Fig. 25). Along its northeastern portion the slump had advanced to the area covered by an adjacent, partly revegetated slump, and here the scarp advanced only a few meters. The upper 40 m of the old slump has numerous parallel fractures separating long turf blocks, indicating extensional flow; this provides a model for how the active slump NOAT159 may continue to evolve over the next few years.

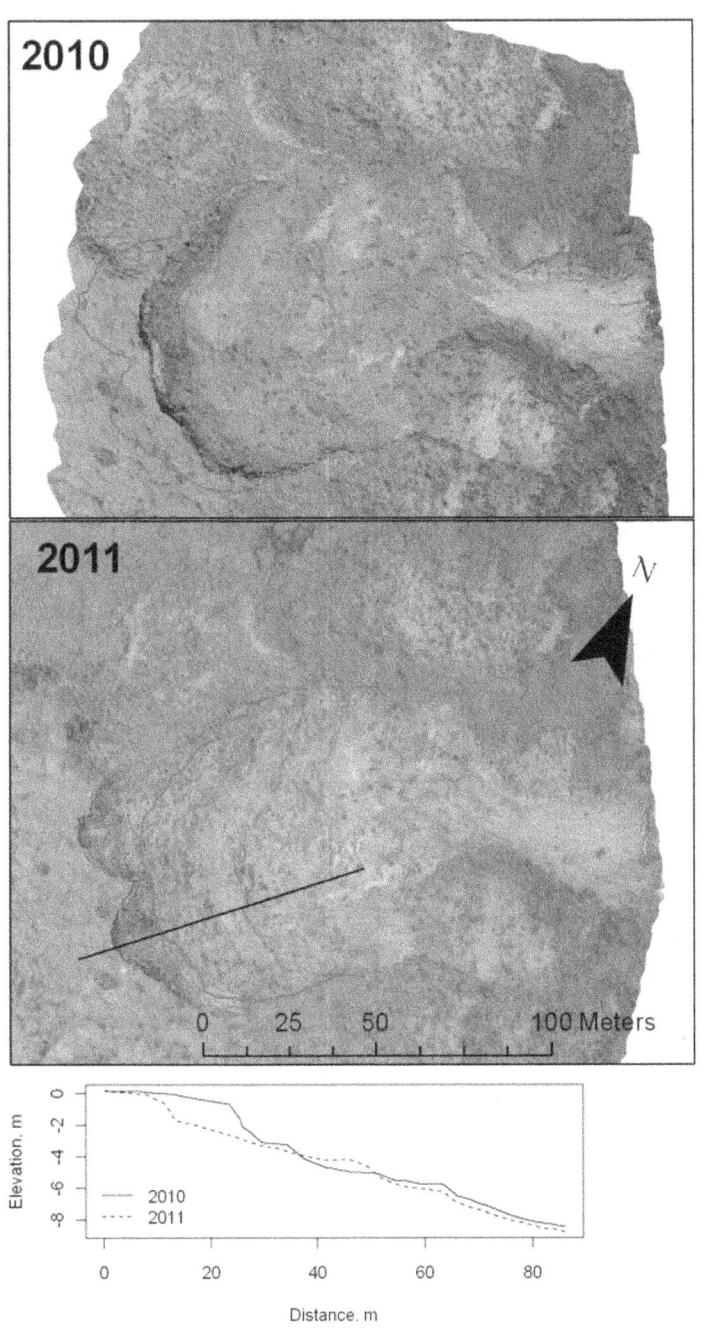

Figure 24. Orthophotographs and cross-sections of slump NOAT159 on 25 June 2010 and 19 July 2011.

Figure 25. Main scarp of slump NOAT159 in 2011. The scarp was 2-3 m high, with no large bodies of ground ice exposed and no extensive zone of liquefied mud. Many large slump blocks have survived the fall down the scarp into the floor of the slump.

NOAT160

NOAT160 displayed modest scarp migration (5-10 m; Fig. 26) as the scarp changed from being partly vertical to dominated by extensional flow (Fig. 27). The amount of volume lost was minor, and there was no significant zone of liquefied mud or accumulation zone of slump material. NOAT160 has reached the top of the local slope, which may retard further growth.

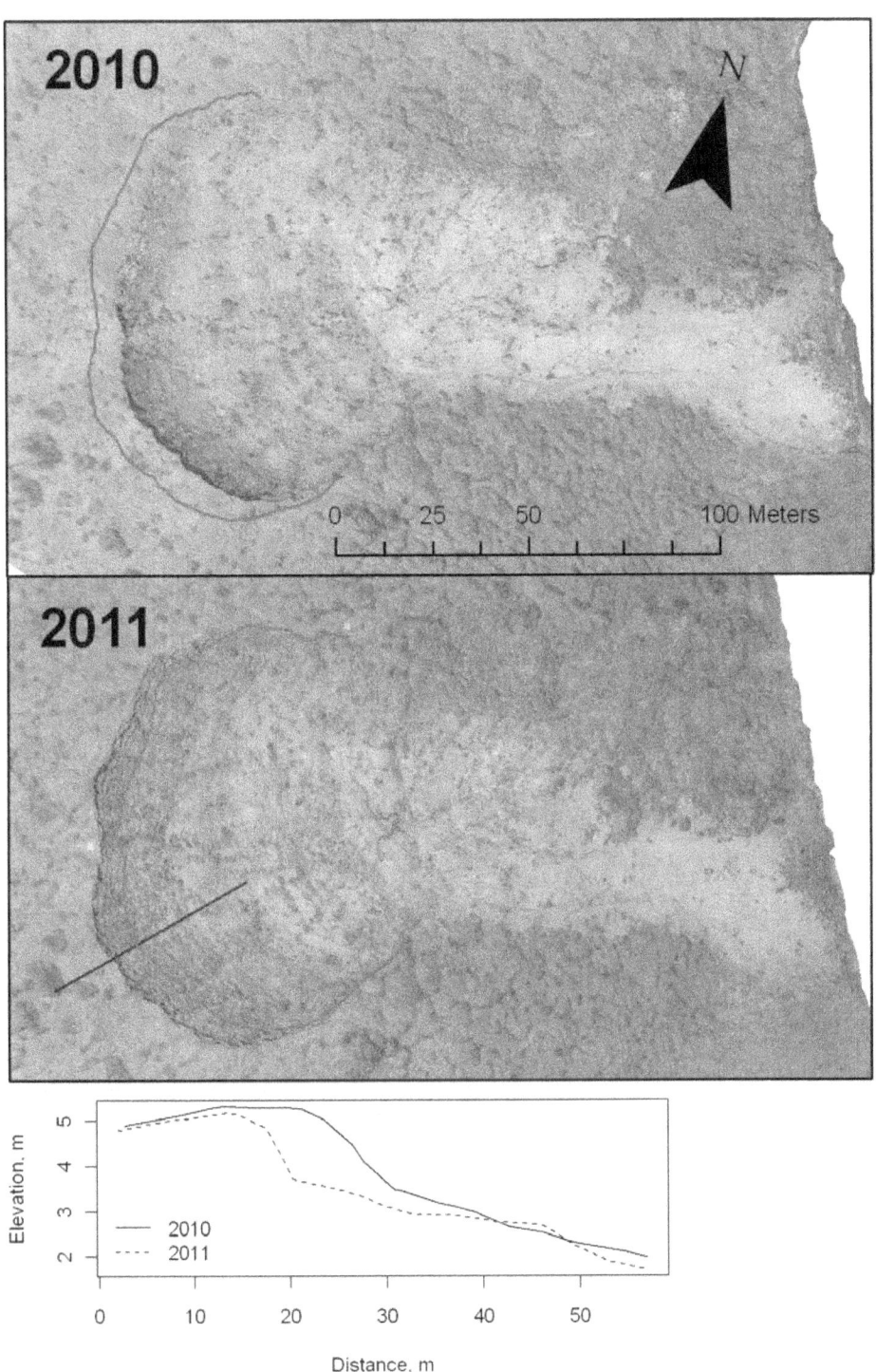

Figure 26. Orthophotographs and cross-sections of slump NOAT160 on 25 June 2010 and 19 July 2011.

33

Figure 27. Main scarp region of slump NOAT160 on 25 June 2010 (upper) and 19 July 2011 (lower). In 2010 the main scarp was still vertical and about 2 m high on the southern (left in the photo) half. Expansion was by extensional flow only on the northern (right) half). By 2011 the whole main scarp was advancing by extensional flow and the scarp was about 1.5 m tall at its highest point.

NOAT161

NOAT161 showed little growth along most of its main scarp, with 1 to 4 m of migration mainly by extensional flow (Fig. 28). The southeastern corner of the slump maintained a nearly vertical scarp with exposed glacial ice, and migrated 20 to 25 m (Fig 29).

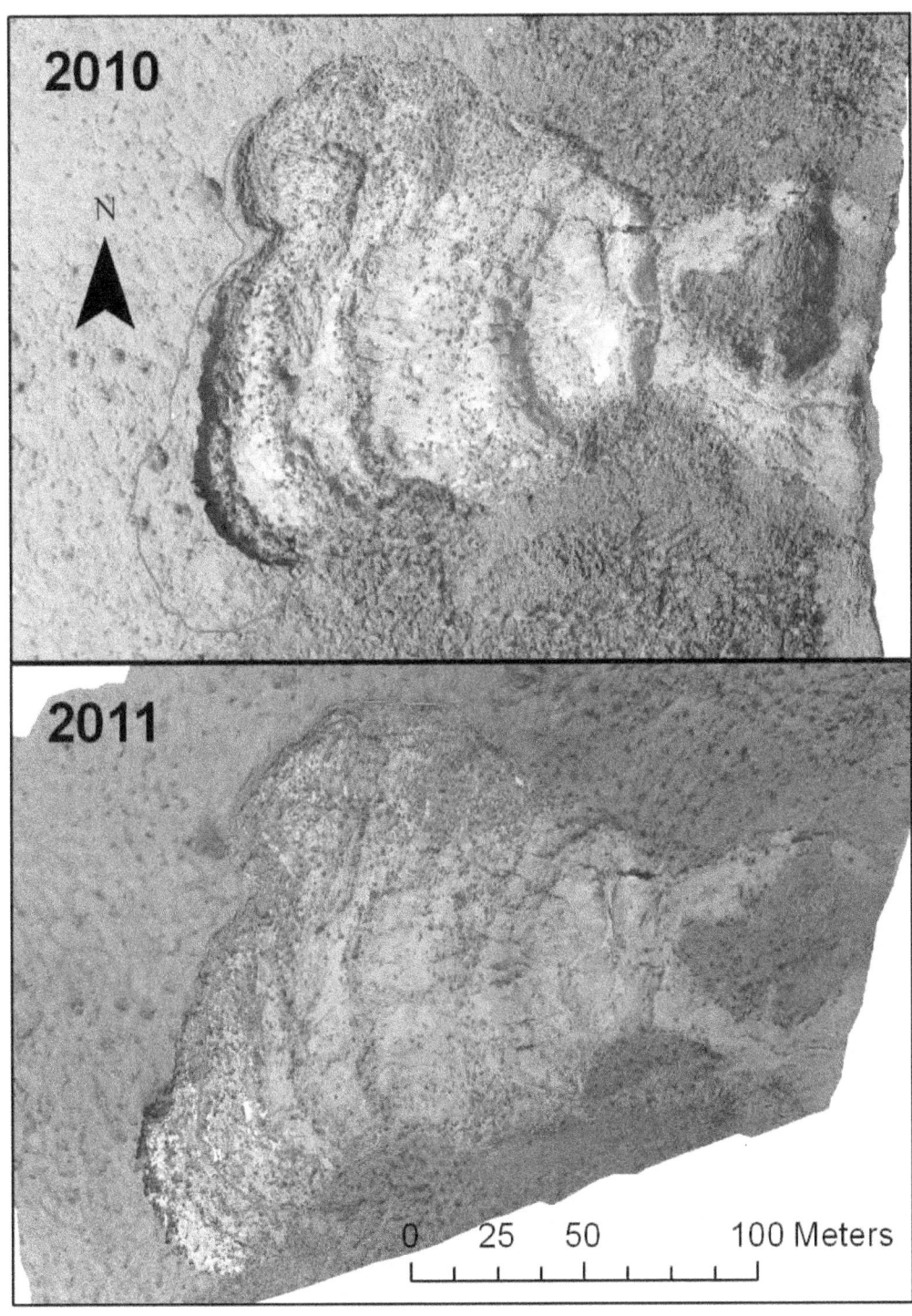

Figure 28. Orthophotographs of slump NOAT161 on 25 June 2010 and 19 July 2011.

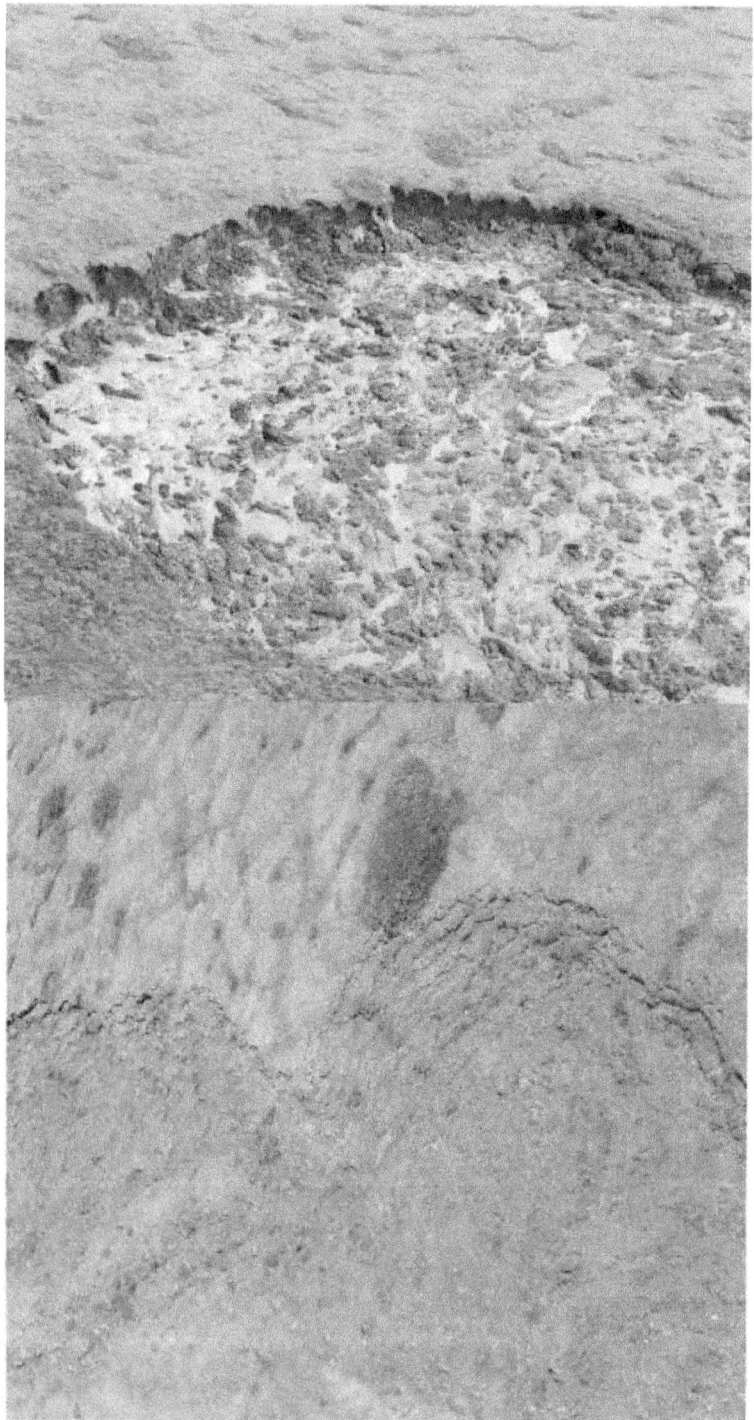

Figure 29. Oblique aerial photographs of the main scarp of slump NOAT161 in 2011. The southeast portion (upper photo) was nearly vertical with glacial till (A) over glacial ice (B). Most of the rest of the main scarp (lower photo) was sloping with extensional flow resulting in numerous parallel cracks in the vegetation mat.

NOAT172

NOAT172 had a tall and vertical main scarp (about 10 m), but the scarp retreated a modest amount (about 10 m). Large Pleistocene ice wedges were observed in the main scarp in 2010, but a laterally extensive buried ice body (e.g., glacial ice) was not observed (Swanson and Hill 2010). The main scarp was not as steep in 2011 as 2010 (Fig. 30), suggesting a trend toward stabilization.

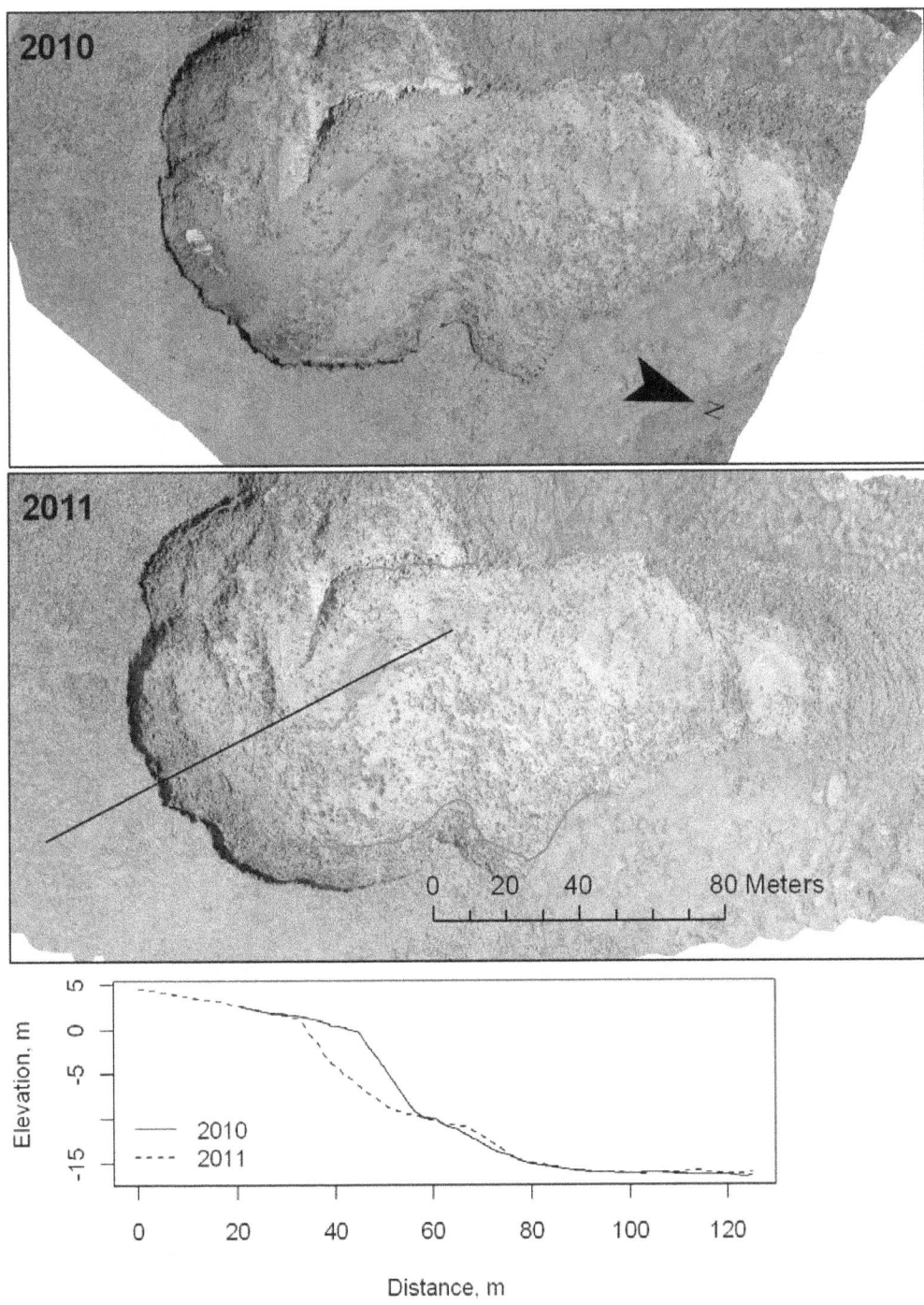

Figure 30. Orthophotographs and cross-sections of slump NOAT172 on 21 June 2010 and 19 July 2011.

37

NOAT237 and NOAT238

These two slumps are in close proximity and were surveyed with one set of control points in 2011 (Fig. 31). They both originated from the shore of a small lake out of the photo to the east (Swanson and Hill 2010). The larger of the two slumps (NOAT237) was more active, adding about 3500 m^2 to the main slump and 250 m^2 to a smaller lobe; the new areas subsided an average of 2.3 m. This slump lost over 10,000 m^3 in the upper subsidence zone, and about one quarter of this volume accumulated just below (Table 2). The main scarp exposed 1.5 to 2 m of glacial till over debris-rich glacial ice (Fig. 32). Slump NOAT238 showed moderate main scarp migration (10 to 20 m) but appeared to be stabilizing: no ice was exposed in the main scarp (Fig. 33) and the floor of the slump was everywhere solid enough to support a person on 18 July 2011.

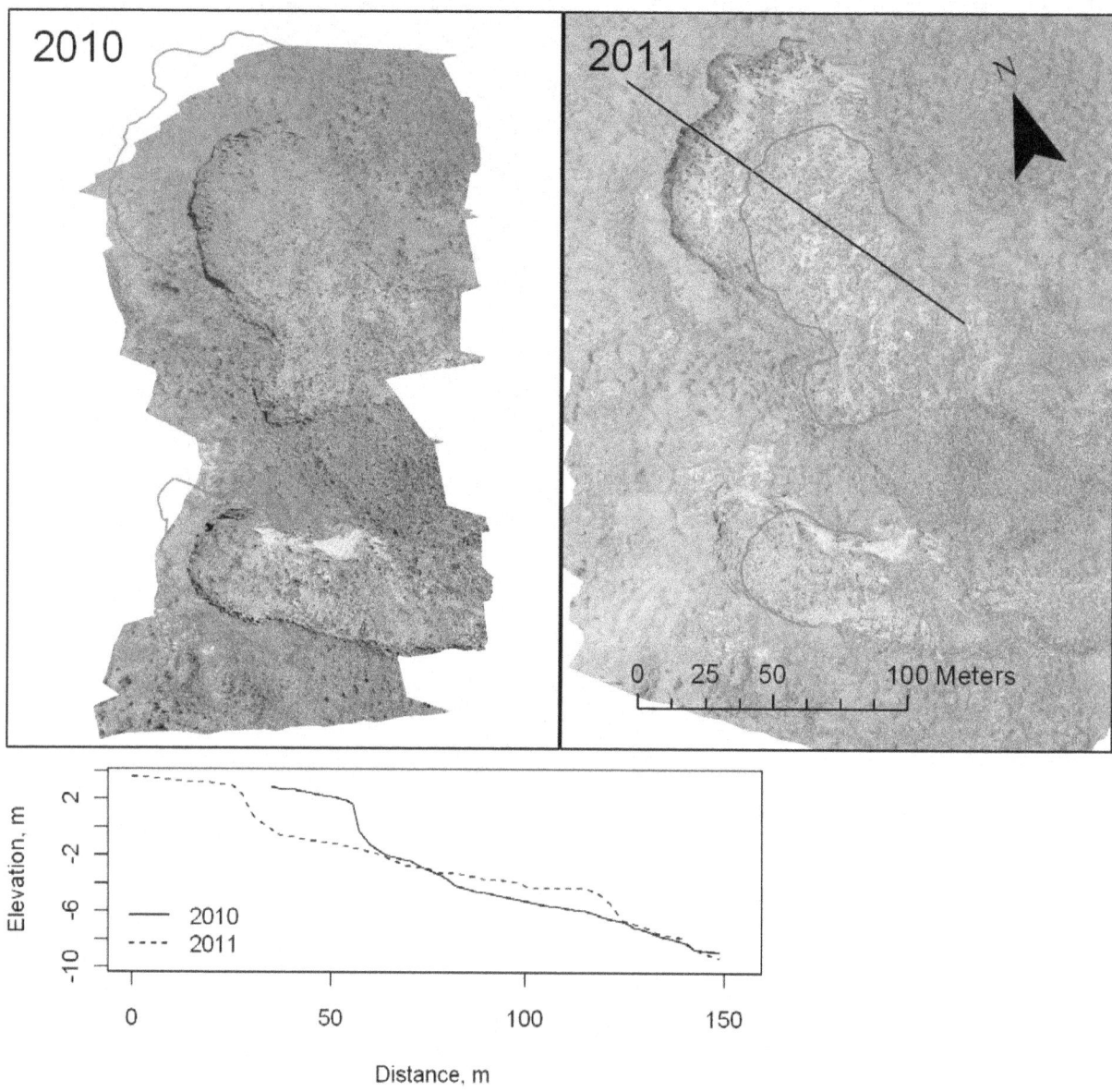

Figure 31. Orthophotographs and cross-sections of slump NOAT237 and NOAT238 on 24 June 2010 and 18 July 2011.

Figure 32. Main scarp of NOAT237 on 18 July 2011. About 1.5 m of glacial till (A) overlies debris-rich glacial ice (B)

Figure 33. Main scarp of NOAT238 on 18 July 2011. The main scarp was completely covered by slump material and there was no liquefied mud zone at the foot of the scarp.

NOAT247 and NOAT248

These two slumps grew very little between 2010 and 2011, with just a few meters of main scarp migration (Fig. 34). The more time-consuming 3-D analysis was not performed for these slumps, because 2-D comparison of the two years revealed little activity. The main scarp over much of its length changed from a sharp-edged cutbank to a rounded slope covered with turf blocks separated by parallel fractures (Fig. 35). This indicates current scarp migration by the extensional flow mechanism, though extensive bare areas on these floors of these slumps suggest that they were recently more active, i.e., had scarps migrating by the "fall and flow" mechanism that destroyed turf blocks.

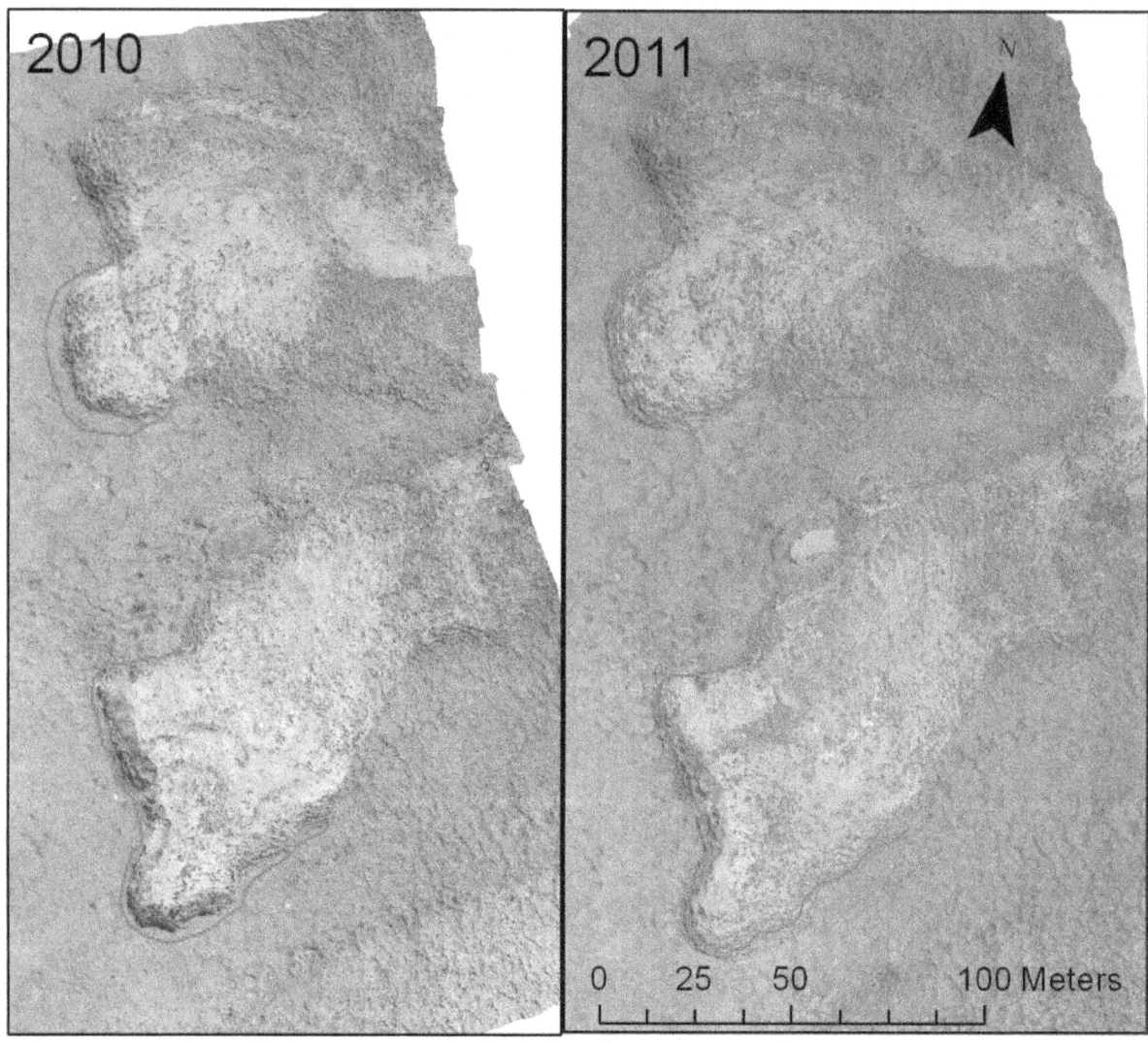

Figure 34. Orthophotographs slumps NOAT247 (lower) and NOAT248 (upper) on 23 June 2010 (left) and 18 July 2011 (right).

Figure 35. Oblique aerial photographs of slump NOAT247, showing the change from a sharp-edged main scarp (2010) to rounded main scarp with long turf blocks separated by parallel fractures (2011). The arrows indicate the positions of three shrubs for reference.

NOAT265

Slump NOAT265 is a large, south-facing slump on a bluff above the Noatak River, photographed and surveyed for the first time in 2011 (Fig. 36). At its highest point the main scarp was just over 20 m high in 2011, the highest escarpment of any retrogressive thaw slump currently known on NPS-administered lands in Alaska. The slump had an area of 30,240 m^2 and the total volume of material lost, based on reconstruction of the slope, was about 138,000 m^3. The area occupied by this slump in 2011 was undisturbed on a 1978 aerial photograph (Fig. 37). Three narrow, partially revegetated disturbed strips extended above the slump; these are active-layer detachments that were quite fresh on the 2008 IKONOS image (Fig. 38). Active-layer detachments are small, shallow landslides over permafrost that form in a few days during exceptionally warm summers (Lewkowicz 2007). The current RTS NOAT265 appears to have started by deep thaw in the lower parts of these active-layer detachments. The main scarp of NOAT265 in July 2011 had migrated about 60 m from its furthest extent in July 2008 (Fig. 38)

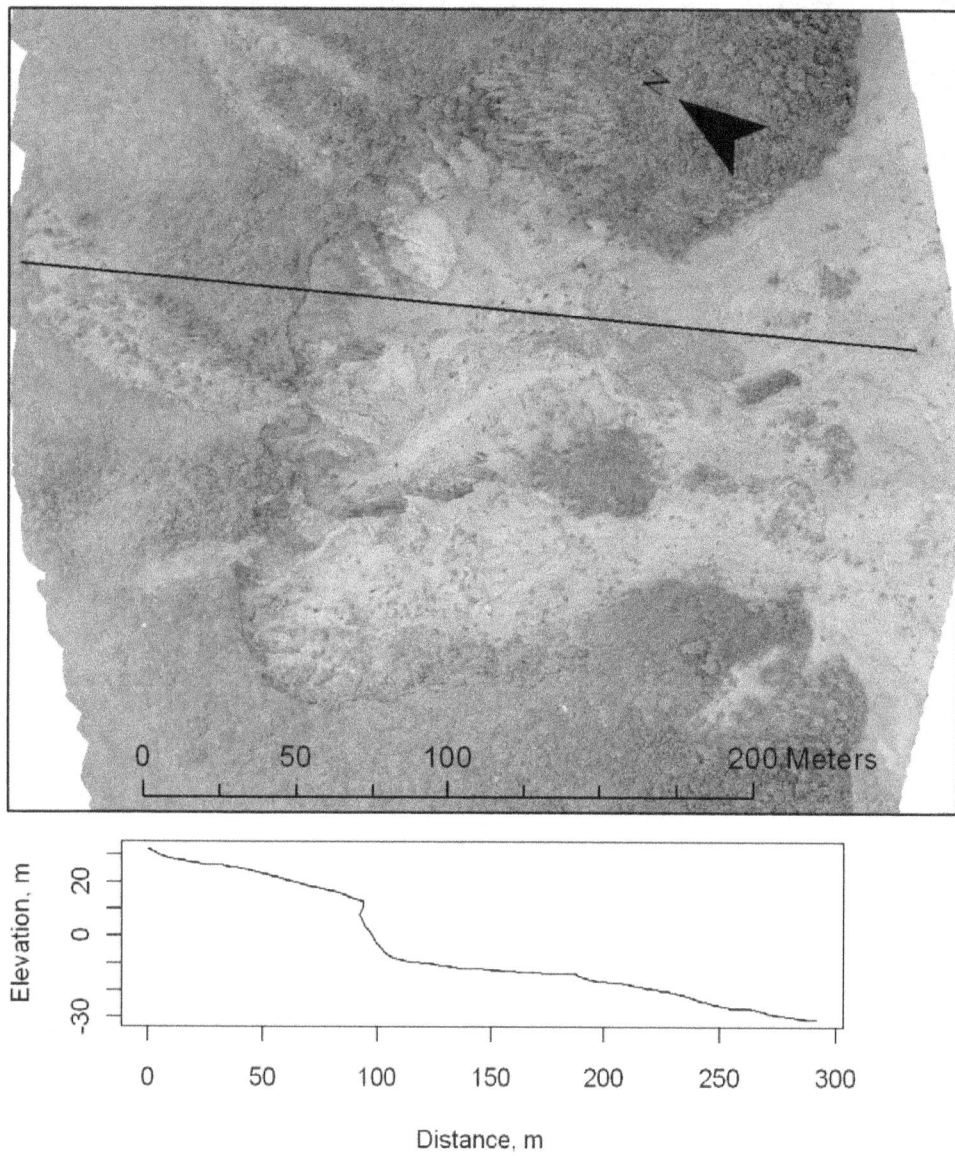

Figure 36. Orthophotograph and cross-section of slump NOAT265, constructed from pass 11F.

42

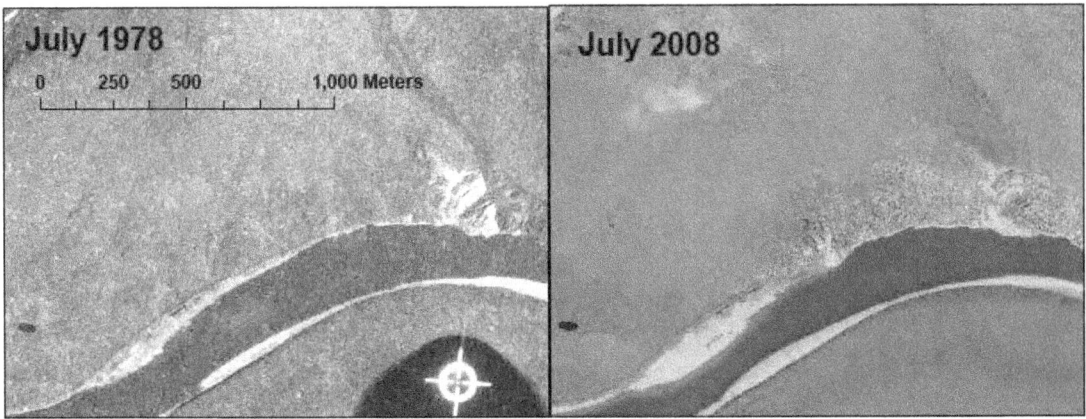

Figure 37. Vicinity of slump NOAT265 in 1978 (left, AHAP aerial photograph) and 2008 (right, IKONOS image). Slump NOAT265 is visible near the center of the 2008 image, but this area was undisturbed in 1978. The bare area near the right edge of both photos is a rotational slide (a deeper geologic mass movement, probably not related to thaw of permafrost; Beltran et al. 1993) that showed little change between the two dates.

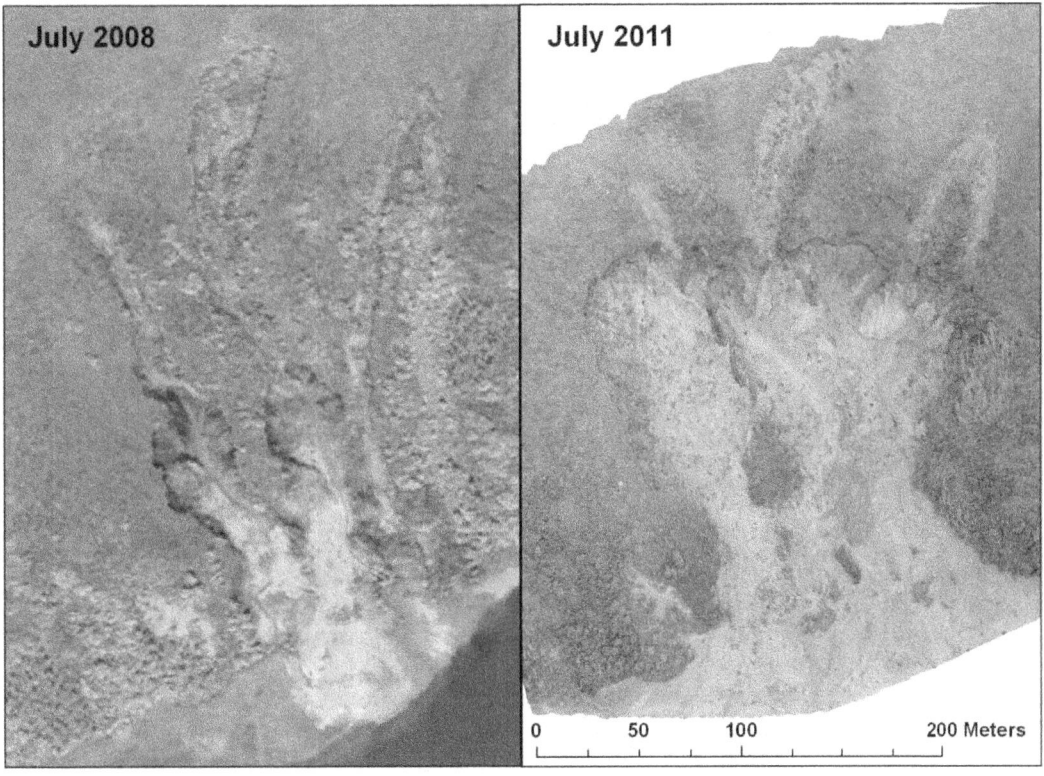

Figure 38. Slump NOAT265 in July of 2008 (IKONOS imagery, 1 m resolution) and July of 2011 (orthophoto from this study). The three bare strips extending above the center of the photo in July of 2008 are active-layer detachments, which had partially revegetated by July 2011.

For comparison, in 2009 the more well-known slump on the Selawik River to the south, which is thought to be the largest in Alaska (Crosby 2009) had a main scarp 10-35 m tall and volume of 540,000 m^3; the main scarp of that slump retreated 35 m from 2007 to 2009, with a volume loss of 187,000 m^3 in 2 yrs.

43

The main scarp of slump NOAT265 exposed sediments unlike any other slumps examined to date. The typical massive ice forms observed in other slumps were not present. Pleistocene ice wedges (present in other slumps with tall main scarps) were lacking, as was the typical sloping mass of debris-rich glacial ice. Very debris-rich glacial may be present (see Fig. 39, B), though this could not be confirmed in the field.

Figure 39. Main scarp of slump NOAT265 on 15 July 2011.). A mixture of coarse- and fine-grained material of glacial origin is visible throughout. The ice-poor material near (A) is typical glacial till or till re-worked by previous slumping. The nature of the material in the face at (B) is uncertain, but it is apparently ice-rich, judging from its thaw to form the liquefied zone below (C); falling debris and lack of solid footing in the mud below prevented close approach.

Discussion

The rapid main scarp migration rates found in the current study (in excess of 20 m between June 2010 and July 2011 at multiple locations) are unprecedented in the literature. They suggest that typical RTS on the order of 100 m to 300 m long could form in less than a decade if the observed rates continued for several years. Meanwhile, some RTS that apparently were quite active in the recent past grew very little between 2010 and 2011. Thus after a burst of growth for a few years, a slump can rather suddenly become quiescent. The implication for monitoring is that we need to be prepared to incorporate into the monitoring program new slumps that show the potential to grow rapidly, as identified by a steep main scarp with exposed ice. Likewise slumps that show less potential for growth, as shown by gentle main scarps without exposed ice, can be revisited less often, e.g., every 2 to 5 years, or dropped from the monitoring program entirely to save time and costs.

Weather data from the closest climate station to the monitored thaw slumps suggest that conditions during the monitoring period were not exceptionally warm, and hence the observed rates of slump growth may be considered typical. Estimated thaw degree-days (computed as monthly mean temperatures times days in the month) were 1119 °C-days and 1000 °C-days for June-July-August 2010 and 2011, respectively at the Noatak RAWS (WRCC 2011), compared to a mean for 1990-2011 (1 year missing) of 1041 °C-days. The two seasons together ranked 9th warmest out of the 19 available consecutive seasons of data, i.e., quite close to the median.

A RTS will become inactive when 1) the mass of ground ice responsible for its growth is exhausted or 2) the overburden cover develops such that it is thicker than the active layer and thus protects the ice from further thaw. Regarding the first cause, we have no information on the thickness of the ice bodies exposed in our slumps, as the bottom contacts of the layers were never observed. Multiple generations of slumps passing over the same area show that stabilization of slumps without exhausting the ice body is common (e.g., slump NOAT151; see also Lantuit and Pollard 2008 and Kokelj et al. 2009).

Some potential mechanisms by which the overburden could thicken to the point where a slump stabilizes include: 1) migration of the main scarp into an area of thicker overburden on the ice mass. For example, if the active layer in bare mud is 1 m and the main scarp migrates into an area with 3 m of overburden, rapid transport of material away from the main scarp would be required to prevent accumulation of a thick overburden, and stabilization is likely. 2) Migration of the main scarp into an area of level slope. This will hinder transport of material away from the scarp and help the overburden build up to active layer thickness. 3) Release of new mineral material from debris-rich ice. We have no data on the debris content of the ice, but melt-out of debris entrained in ice was the original source of most of the material we see on top of glacial ice in moraines today, and it is presumably still a significant source. 4) Thinning of the active layer due to variations in weather. The active layer varies from year to year in response to variations in temperature and snow depth, and if the active layer became thinner this could stabilize a slump.

Climate change could change the scenario for slump stabilization in the future. We currently lack ground temperatures from the study area, but know from the weather stations cited previously that mean annual air temperatures range from about -4° C in the west to about -8° C in the east. Projections of climate warming in NOAT in the future (SNAP 2009) are about 3° C by the year

2040 and 6° C by 2080. Permafrost temperatures are typically 1° to 5° C warmer than the mean annual air temperature. Thus the projected degree of warming could bring permafrost temperatures to near or above freezing, first in the west and then throughout the study area. If this were to occur, then the active layer on un-vegetated surfaces would become very thick, or permafrost would be destabilized entirely, such that RTS expansion would cease only after consumption of all the ground ice.

Most of the slumps studied here showed significant volume loss in the upper zone of new subsidence, and a lesser volume of material accumulated just below. The missing volume is probably ice that melted and ran off, and to a lesser extent sediment transported away in runoff. The accumulation zones extended no more than about 50 m downslope from the subsidence zone, and the older, lower parts of the slumps were largely stable.

We failed to observe the formation of the fans of debris that are present below most of the slumps. Perhaps these fans 1) form during infrequent extreme events (e.g., a spring after a big snow year, or in the summer after unusually heavy rain), or 2) they form mainly in the early part of a slump's development, when there is as yet no extensive slump floor where the liquefied mud released by thaw can gradually dewater while moving slowly downslope. In other words, at early stages in the slump's formation the liquefied mud spills rapidly over vegetation below the slump or directly into the adjacent water body, while later in the slump's evolution the liquefied mud dewaters and stabilizes on the slump floor.

Literature Cited

Balser, A. W. W. B. Bowden, J. B. Jones, M. N. Gooseff, D. M. Sanzone, A. Bouchier, and A. Allen, 2007. Thermokarst distribution in the Noatak Basin, Alaska: increased frequency and correlations with local and regional landscape variables. American Geophysical Union, Fall Meeting 2007, abstract #C32A-08.

Beltran, L., D. M. Cruden, E. Krauter, G. Lefèvre, G. I. Ter-Stepanian, and Z. Zhouyuan. 1993. Multilingual landslide glossary. The International Geotechnical Societies' UNESCO Working Party for World Landslide Inventory. Bi-Tech Publishers, Richmond, B.C. Canada. 50 pp. Available from: http://www.cgs.ca/pdf/heritage/Landslide%20Glossary.pdf (accessed 29 Dec 2011).

Bowden, W. B., M. N. Gooseff, A. Balser, A. Green, B. J. Peterson, and J. Bradford. 2008. Sediment and nutrient delivery from thermokarst features in the foothills of the North Slope, Alaska: Potential impacts on headwater stream ecosystems. Journal of Geophysical Research, Vol. 113, G02026, 12 pp

Burn, C. R., and A. G. Lewkowicz. 1990. Retrogressive thaw slumps. Canadian landform examples – 17. The Canadian Geographer 34(3):273–276.

Crosby, B. T. 2009. The interplay between storage and delivery: an examination of temporally varying sediment flux to the Selawik River from an enormous retrogressive thaw slump, northwest Alaska. Geological Society of America Abstracts with Programs, Vol. 41, No. 7, p. 574.

Hamilton, T. D. 2010. Surficial geologic map of the Noatak National Preserve. Scientific Investigations Map 3036. U.S. Geological Survey, Federal Center, Colorado, scale 1:250,000.

Jorgenson, M. T., Y. L. Shur, and E. R. Pullman. 2006. Abrupt increase in permafrost degradation in Alaska. Geophysical Research Letters 33:L02503.

Jorgenson, T., K. Yoshikawa, M. Kanevskiy, Y. Shur, V. Romanovsky, S. Marchenko, G. Grosse, J. Brown, and B. Jones. 2008. Permafrost characteristics of Alaska. Proceedings of the Ninth International Conference on Permafrost. University of Alaska Fairbanks, Institute of Northern Engineering.

Kanevskiy, M., Y. Shur, D. Fortier, M. T. Jorgenson, and E. Stephani. 2011. Cryostratigraphy of late Pleistocene syngenetic permafrost (yedoma) in northern Alaska, Itkillik River exposure. Quaternary Research 75:584-596.

Kokelj, S. V., R. E. Jenkins, D. Milburn, C. R. Burn, and N. Snow. 2005. The influence of thermokarst disturbance on the water quality of small upland lakes, Mackenzie Delta region, Northwest Territories, Canada. Permafrost and Periglacial Processes 16:343-353.

Kokelj, S. V., T. C. Lantz, J. Kanigan, S. L. Smith, and R. Coutts. 2009. Origin and polycyclic behavior of tundra thaw slumps, Mackenzie Delta region, Northwest Territories, Canada. Permafrost and Periglacial Processes 20:173-184.

Lacelle, D., J. Bjornson, and B. Lauriol. 2010. Climatic and geomorphic factors affecting contemporary (1950-2004) activity of retrogressive thaw slumps on the Aklavik Plateau, Richardson Mountains, NWT, Canada. Permafrost and Periglacial Processes 21:1-15.

Lantz, T. C., and S. V. Kokelj. 2008. Increasing rates of retrogressive thaw slump activity in the Mackenzie Delta region, N.W.T., Canada. Geophysical Research Letters 35, L06502, 5 pp.

Lantuit, H., and W. H. Pollard. 2008. Fifty years of coastal erosion and retrogressive thaw slump activity on Herschel Island, southern Beaufort Sea, Yukon Territory, Canada. Geomorphology 95:84-102.

Lawler, J. P., S. D. Miller, D. M. Sanzone, J. Ver Hoef, and S. B. Young. 2009. Arctic network vital signs monitoring plan. Natural Resource Report NPS/ARCN/NRR-2009/088. U.S. Department of the Interior, National Park Service, Natural Resource Program Center, Ft. Collins, Colorado.

Lewkowicz, A. G. 2007. Dynamics of active-layer detachments failures, Fosheim Peninsula, Ellesmere Island, Nunavut, Canada. Permafrost and Periglacial Processes 18:89-103.

Murton, J. B., C. A. Whiteman, R. I. Waller, W. H. Pollard, I. D. Clarke, and S. R. Dallimore. 2005. Basal ice facies and supraglacial melt-out till of the Laurentide Ice Sheet, Tuktoyaktuk Coastlands, western Arctic Canada. Quaternary Science Reviews 24:681-708.

Scenarios Network for Alaska Planning (SNAP). 2009. Projected climate change scenarios for Noatak National Preserve. http://snap.uaf.edu/files/docs/Climate_Change_Sums/Noatak_ClimSum.pdf (accessed 16 Nov 2011).

Swanson, D. K., and K. Hill. 2010. Monitoring of retrogressive thaw slumps in the Arctic Network, 2010 baseline data: Three-dimensional modeling with small-format aerial photographs. Natural Resource Data Series NPS/ARCN/NRDS—2010/123. National Park Service, Fort Collins, Colorado.

Swanson, D. K. 2012. Mapping of erosion features related to thaw of permafrost in Noatak National Preserve. Natural Resource Data Series NPS/ARCN/NRDS—2012/248. National Park Service, Fort Collins, Colorado.

Western Regional Climate Center (WRCC). 2011. RAWS USA climate archives. http://www.raws.dri.edu/wraws/akF.html (accessed 12 April 2011).